THE TYLENOL MURDERS

A FATHER'S CONFESSION TO HIS SON

JOSEPH CIBELLI

WILD BLUE PRESS

WildBluePress.com

THE TYLENOL MURDERS published by:
WILDBLUE PRESS
P.O. Box 102440
Denver, Colorado 80250

WILDBLUE PRESS is registered at the U.S. Patent and Trademark Offices.

ISBN 978-1-970361-08-7 Hardcover
ISBN 978-1-970361-09-4 Trade Paperback
ISBN 978-1-970361-07-0 eBook

Interior Formatting and Book Cover Design by Elijah Toten
www.totencreative.com

THE TYLENOL MURDERS

Daniel Raymond Drozd. Circa 1982.

PROLOGUE

When a loved one is lost, the pain doesn't end with silence or burial. It ripples, spreading slowly and indiscriminately through generations, through memories, through the delicate webs of relationships that tether us to one another. Like a stone thrown into still water, the initial impact is sudden, jarring. But the waves that follow are more insidious. They touch everything. And they last far longer.

My family, like many, has borne the weight of unspoken trauma. Layer upon layer, secret upon secret, packed so tightly that none of us could fully see the shape of it until we were already drowning in its aftermath. For years, I lived under the shadow of my father, never fully understanding what that shadow concealed. Now, I know. And knowing has changed me forever.

My father wasn't only a complex man. He was a dark man. His shadow wasn't by chance or mistake. He engineered it. He weaponized it. He designed pain with precision. He walked corridors of cruelty that no child should have to follow. His strategies weren't impulsive. They were deliberate. They were honed through psychopathy. They were reinforced through narcissistic entitlement. They were sharpened by antisocial rage. I discovered truths no son should learn. I traced footsteps no child should be forced to see. I unearthed cruelty so intricate that it defied belief.

I didn't begin this journey to write a book. I began it to understand. I sought the truth for the families. I sought the truth for the victims. I sought the truth for ghosts that still whispered. I needed to see what had happened. I needed to face what I had lived inside. Yet along the way, I became more than a seeker. I became a vessel. I carried the pathology of my father until I could set it down. What I uncovered wasn't merely crime. It was legacy. It was a curse. It was a sickness disguised as silence and malice.

This man, my father, was sick. That cannot be denied. In one of his hands, he destroyed. In the other hand, he held mine as a child. There is no script for grieving such a man. There is no map for mourning someone who murdered trust itself. I don't excuse him. I don't justify him. I only understand now what he was. And in that understanding, I find a kind of forgiveness. Not for him. For myself. For the questions that went unasked. For the dots that I failed to connect in time. For the blindness that lasted too long.

To the families of the victims, I wasn't guilty, yet I carry the weight of proximity. I carry the shame of silence. I carry the inheritance of his shadow. I cannot erase grief. I cannot undo years of chaos and manipulation. I can only speak. His genius lay not only in destruction. It lay in disguise. Now, at last, that disguise is gone.

This book is the reckoning. This book is the closure. This book is the confrontation. I tell this story not because I wish to, but because I must. Some truths demand air. Some truths, once unearthed, cannot be buried again. My heart aches for the stolen lives. My heart aches for the innocence destroyed. My heart aches for the child I was, lost in his labyrinth. Yet in the aching, there is rhythm. In the rhythm, there is resolve. The ripples don't end here. The ripples have a name.

PREFACE

The Tylenol Murders: A Father's Confession to His Son is a true crime memoir told in two voices: the terrified clarity of an 11-year-old child and the measured precision of the man he became.

Through a child's eyes, the story begins with the unease of living under a shadow that cannot be named. Ordinary suburban days twist into something darker: strange rituals, chilling silences, cryptic mutterings, and excursions that never feel safe. The boy senses danger without possessing the language to define it. He records the smell of surroundings, the sharp snap of a bottle cap, the cold sting of fear in his stomach.

Decades later, that boy is a man trained in the law and forensic psychology. With years of legal study and clinical knowledge under his belt, he returns to those memories and reevaluates them with hard-edged clarity. What once seemed like odd behavior becomes evidence of pathology. Where he once felt only dread, he now sees manipulation, psychopathy, and a disturbing alignment with one of America's most infamous crimes.

The story begins not with a sunny, happy afternoon, but with a chilling echo. On his deathbed, the figure at the center of suspicion offered not a confession, but a declaration. Words that froze the room and confirmed the boy's lifelong fear that the darkness he sensed was never imagined. It was real. It was deliberate. It was claimed.

This isn't a retelling of headlines. It's testimony from inside the orbit of a madman, reinterpreted through the dual lenses of witness testimony and expertise. *The Tylenol Murders: A Father's Confession to His Son* is a memoir, a case study, and a reckoning. It analyzes not only who could commit such acts, but what becomes of a child who grows up under their shadow.

FOREWORD

Joseph Cibelli is a writer, legal student, and forensic psychology PhD whose life and work sit at the intersection of law, psychology, and lived experience. After more than three decades as a successful salon owner and entrepreneur, he turned his focus to higher education.

He completed a Bachelor of Science in Criminal Justice before entering law school. He is now a third-year Juris Doctor candidate and, in parallel, he just finished a PhD in Forensic Psychology, with research aimed at bridging clinical insight and the courtroom.

Cibelli's path is unique, from salon chair to lecture hall. Witness to survivor. A student of both statutes and minds, he infuses his work with an uncommon perspective. His writing draws from a lifetime of observation sharpened by legal training and forensic study, crafting narratives that are both deeply personal and rigorously analytical.

The Tylenol Murders: A Father's Confession to His Son is his debut book, a true crime memoir told through the dual lenses of childhood memory and professional expertise. It's the culmination of decades of reflection, study, and reckoning with a past shadowed by one of America's largest mass murders.

Cibelli's mission, in both scholarship and storytelling, is to foster a more people-centered system of law and to shed light on the psychological dimensions of justice. He lives in California with his husband Craig, and continues to write at the confluence of law, psychology, and memory.

This column was originally published in the Chicago Tribune on October 18, 1982.[1]

Dear Madman,

If you are the Tylenol killer, some of this may matter to you. Or it may make no difference at all.

If you are the Tylenol killer, your whole murderous exercise may have seemed beautiful in the flawlessness of its execution. You doctored the capsules, and the people died, and you put fear in hearts all over the nation. If you are the killer, the success of your mission may be sustaining you.

If you are the Tylenol killer, though, you may be harboring just the vaguest curiosity about the people on the other end of your plan: the people who were unfortunate enough to purchase the bottles you had touched.

If you are curious, come to a small house on a quiet, winding street in Elk Grove Village. Come to 1425 Armstrong Lane. The people who live there, Dennis and Jeanna Kellerman, feel you have already been inside anyway.

---

1. Bob Greene, "Dear Madman," *Chicago Tribune*, October 18, 1982

Mary Kellerman, 12, was the first of seven victims who died after ingesting cyanide-laced Tylenol capsules Sept. 29, 1982, in Elk Grove Village.

Maybe the names don't mean anything to you. You killed their daughter. She was 12; her name was Mary Kellerman, and her crime was that she had a cold.

You might be interested in hearing what you have done to her parents. They are still numb, alone in the house. Jeanna Kellerman blames herself. You see, she came home from work on the day before her daughter died, and on the way she stopped to pick up some medicine. Mary was a child who didn't like to take medication; she would go "yuck" when her mother offered her cough syrup.

So on that afternoon Mrs. Kellerman purchased a new bottle of cough syrup with a flavor that Mary might like a little better. And she picked up a bottle of Tylenol, too. At first she was going to buy a small bottle; then, because she suffers from arthritis, and she thought she might need a pill soon, she changed her mind and bought the next bigger size.

She bought your bottle.

You ought to see her now, crying, her eyes vacant, as she sits in the family living room and talks about what her life might be like if only she had stuck with the first bottle that afternoon.

You might be interested in Mary's father, too. He woke up the next morning and went into Mary's room. She told him that her throat was so sore. He said he wanted her to stay home from school.

He remembers exactly:

"I heard her go into the bathroom. I heard the door close. Then I heard something drop. I went to the bathroom door. I called, 'Mary, are you okay?' There was no answer. I called again: 'Mary, are you okay?' There was still no answer. So I opened the bathroom door, and my little girl was on the floor unconscious. She was still in her pajamas."

You might be interested in knowing that when Mary's mother and father returned from the hospital. Returned without Mary, who, as you know, was dead. They looked in the refrigerator. In the refrigerator was a brown paper sack with a sandwich and a piece of pie inside. Mary had packed her lunch the night before. She thought she would be going to school, so she made herself the sandwich. She could not have known about you.

On the front of that refrigerator are a number of funny, furry little animals with magnets fastened to their backs. They are used to attach notes to the refrigerator door. Maybe you would care: Mary made those for her mother. They were gifts.

If you are wondering whether Mary's parents talk about you, you don't have to wonder anymore. They do. You have never been in their house, and yet they cannot walk into a room without feeling you are there. You don't know them, but you have changed their lives forever; they feel as if they can't get away from you. If you had only wanted to steal their car, they think; if you had only wanted to burn down their house. Anything; they would have said yes to anything.

Anything but this.

Do you want to know what they are thinking about you? "I would pay anything if whoever did this would walk up to my door right now." That's what Mary's father said. "I would give everything I own. Because once he walks into that door, he's mine."

As it is, you should know, Mary's parents are too shattered to even visit the cemetery. Mary is buried at St. Michael the Archangel in Palatine, and they wish they could go to her grave. But they can't; the hurt is too deep, and you are keeping them even from that.

If you are the Tylenol killer, you should know one more thing:

Mary's mother can't have any more children. Mary was her only baby; you might be interested in knowing that Mary was born one month premature, and that as she entered the world her mother was scared because she was not crying. But the doctor smiled and said, "It's all right; she's only sleeping." And she was; she was a quiet child, and because the Kellermans knew she would be their only child, she was especially precious to them.

You should know that Mary's mother has not gone into Mary's bedroom since her daughter died. Her clothes are still there, and her school books and papers. The door is closed; Mary's mother and father have to walk past it every time they go upstairs. Mary's father has gone inside, but just once; he went in to pick out the clothes for Mary to wear at her funeral.

If you are the Tylenol killer, you might want to know that Mary's parents always considered themselves to be overly protective. Mary always had to be home by dark; even when she was out with friends, she had to call home frequently just to say she was all right.

The reason Mary's parents were like that was that they knew something that a 12-year-old girl couldn't know. They knew that the world can at times be a cruel place, and that parents have a duty to protect their child from dangers the child might not even know are there.

They thought they knew about every danger that could possibly touch Mary.

But they did not know about you.

SEPTEMBER 29, 2023

Forty-one years to the day after seven unsuspecting souls were poisoned by a faceless killer, my father, Daniel Raymond Drozd, lay dying in the quiet familiarity of my childhood home. His body was ravaged by pancreatic cancer, each breath a tremoring testament to mortality. Hospice bore witness. Death hovered, patient and vast.

He drifted in and out of sleep. The drugs loosened him. His guard slipped. His mind cracked open just enough for his secrets to leak out. It started with a whisper. A half-formed murmur. Words sliding out before he could cage them.

"Cyanide pills… I did it."

Phil Collins was playing softly in the background: *In the Air Tonight.*

A song about waiting. About knowing. About seeing something terrible and choosing silence. A song with heavy promise. With dread. With inevitability.

A final perverse flourish. His last act wasn't an act of contrition. It was a performance. A madman's insistence.

He froze. His expression collapsed. He stared with a sorrow so heavy it seemed to press the air flat. He whispered, "I'm tired. I need to sleep." He turned away. His shoulders trembled. The sound of quiet crying drifted across the room.

Sleep gently came to him, but only for a few seconds. He awoke. His voice shook. His face twisted. His eyes pointed toward something far beyond the room. Something beyond time. Something he carried alone. He asked, "What did I say?" His breath quickened. Panic surfaced. He waited for an answer that never came.

The medication dragged him deeper. His control dissolved once again. His voice returned, thin and cracked.

He uttered in a voice just barely audible, "The three Marys should still be here. One of them was so young."

The song continued. Low. Ominous. A reminder that some moments announce themselves long before they arrive.

Again, staring into another dimension, he uttered to some unknown entity, "If *you* knew it was true, what I did. If *you* didn't do anything about it. *You* should be ashamed of yourself. *You* would be the monster."

When clarity returned, his eyes hardened. He delivered a warning to the others in the room.

He said he would get blamed. He said blame would come someday. He said someone would point at him. His voice lowered to a rasp.

"It might be a year. It might be ten years. Or it might never happen, but I'm going to be blamed for something terrible, so I will just admit it now."

He stared straight ahead. The words felt rehearsed. A preemptive strike. A man arguing with a future accuser. A man terrified of a truth that would surface, a truth that he unearthed himself.

Exhaustion had filled the marrow in his bones. All of this dialogue had worn him out again.

But he suddenly broke forth.

His body shook. His breath stuttered. His jaw clenched tight. He whispered through teeth that barely parted, and for a second time, he clearly exclaimed,

"Cyanide pills… I did it. It was me."

The room froze around him. The air thickened. His words hung there like a toxic gas. He spiraled deeper into whatever truth lived inside him. A truth shaped like guilt. A truth shaped like death. A truth shaped like three Marys. A truth that smelled of bitter almond.

In legal doctrine, words uttered on the brink of death can carry extraordinary weight. A dying declaration may pierce the hearsay rule, even when untested by cross-examination, because the law presumes that one who is dying speaks truth, owing to lack of motive to lie and a settled expectation of death. But this was no solemn admission. These truths were delivered as a spectacle.

Silence crashed into the room as he collapsed back into the bed. Fading. Not yet gone. Not still present. To others, these might have seemed to be delirium's last stubborn breath. To me, they were confirmation. Statements trailing death but not born of fear. Born, rather, of pride. Confessions wrapped in narcissism and cruelty. Impending death made the statements unavailable to cross-examination, yet they landed with clarity. No denial could withstand them. These were a few of the last words ever spoken by Daniel Raymond Drozd, my father.

Three Marys.

A looming blame.

A confession soaked in cyanide.

Everything pointed inward.

Everything pointed back.

In that split second, decades of fragmented memories clicked into place. His psychopathic orchestration of pain, his narcissistic command of control, his antisocial disregard, all of it crystallized in those few sentences. He left behind no apology. Only a challenge. A curse. A legal ghost was thrown into my lap.

I carry this story through the eyes of an 11-year-old. Confused, terrified, weighed with something I couldn't yet name. I have chosen every word here with surgical care. These pages are evidence. These pages are truth demanded, not given.

So, I turn to you, the reader. Step with me back in time. Step into 1982, when medicine wasn't sealed. When there was no 24/7 news cycle. View this story through my youthful eyes, then through my lens today—armed with legal analysis, psychological training, and clarity. This isn't recollection. This is evidence. This is the reckoning he forced upon me. Something truly was in the air.

These words were no dying confession. They were his final, defiant testament. And they marked the beginning of a journey into the madness he engineered.

My father spoke in riddles.
My father spoke in rhymes.
He trained me in the silence;
To erase tracks and time.

"Stay left," he'd say, "look upward.
Trust nothing that you hear."
We hunted humans through wooded trails,
Like ghosts, they'd never fear.

He showed me how to read the land,
To breathe without a sound.
To stalk them through the underbrush,
And leave no trace on ground.

He taught me ciphers, taught me codes,
And lies behind the face,
To study every weakness
And vanish without trace.

He was a man of secrets,
A man who knew no peace.
Poison was his chosen weapon,
Darkness his release.

These are my truths,
Truths I cannot undo.
Not stories made to comfort,
But what the shadows knew.

Joseph Cibelli

SECTION ONE

CHAPTER ONE: THE BEGINNING OF THE END

1981

January arrived with a vengeance, Chicago style. Bitter cold, endless snow, howling blizzards. But inside our home, the real storm had already begun to churn. My mom was pregnant, and while that should have meant joy, something deeper stirred in me, a strange mix of anticipation and terror. It was as if another soul was being ushered into a collapsing house with no exits.

Outside, the world was frozen. Inside, it was catching fire.

The violence wasn't new but was escalating. My father's meltdowns grew louder, more frequent. Like tectonic shifts in our small house, the outbursts cracked through the walls. My mom, pregnant and fragile, was still his preferred target, but we all shared the blows in one way or another. My brother bore them physically, thrown down the basement steps. I can still hear the thuds, the screams echoing, glass Royal Crown Cola bottles shattering on concrete. It was chaos. Predictable in its horror, yet each time felt worse than the last.

I wasn't even 10 years old yet, but my education in survival was already in full session. Fight, flight, or freeze. Those are the three primal choices humans are hardwired to make in the face of a threat. Freezing had never worked for me. The few times I tried to disappear into silence or stillness, it only made me a quieter, easier target. So, I stopped freezing. Flight wasn't an option either. Where was there to go? We were locked in a prison of snowdrifts and secrets. That left one choice.

Fight.

I started to fight back. Not with fists yet, but with eyes, with will, with a quiet vow that I wouldn't let this monster crush us all.

My brother, Justin, was just a toddler, and mischief defined him. He vanished one afternoon, and the house erupted in a frantic search. Every room was combed. Every closet was checked. We found him on the bathroom floor, his small body folded in front of the vanity cabinet. In his hands was an open bottle of children's liquid Tylenol. Syrupy red medicine was dripping onto the tile.

My father stormed in. He snatched Justin up, rage exploding. The rest of the bottle spilled across the floor. Sticky, crimson. Spreading slowly like blood. Dan's foot slipped in the slick mess as he pulled Justin hard against his chest.

Then he pounded. Heavy blows across Justin's back, as if Justin were choking. As if he were suffocating, though his airway was clear. My father's face twisted, not with fear for his son, but with something older. His mind was reliving another bathroom, another day, another bottle. He had been barely older than Justin. A curious boy, he was scavenging under his grandmother's sink. He had found a bottle too. Liquid medicine, long forgotten. Sweet on the tongue. Red like cherries. Or maybe raspberries. He drank it down. The medicine contained sulfa, a drug made from synthetic sulfur. A drug that triggers violent immune reactions in those allergic to it. Once used as a precursor of modern-day antibiotics, this once miracle drug turned deadly for Dan. His body turned traitor. He collapsed. He was hospitalized for weeks. He later told me he died that day. That he was brought back. That he never returned whole.

That memory never left him. It haunted every bottle of medication. Every pill on every shelf. What spilled on our bathroom floor wasn't just medication. It was his trauma resurrected. It was poison, betrayal, and death all flooding back in a single instant. He struck Justin's back as if punishing the child for trespassing into his own past. His mind collapsed in time. His son became himself. His fear became violence. His trauma became a weapon.

He told me later that he had crossed over that day in his grandmother's house. That he had tasted death and returned altered. That he had been given back, yet never as he once was. His words came with pride, as if that brush with death excused what came after. As if that day explained why the darkness had the right to grow inside him.

In a manic frenzy, he left the house. Went to the hardware store and came home with childproof latches for all of the cabinets in the house. It was his mission that day to prevent what had happened to him that day back in the 1950s. The day he was poisoned and died.

Then came July 15, 1981. My sister, Elizabeth Grace, was born just two days before my tenth birthday. A girl. A miracle. Another sibling to love. Another life to try and protect.

But even her arrival couldn't slow the descent. In fact, things were accelerating now. My mom made a brave move: she enrolled in nursing school. There were whispers that she had finally decided to break free. To build a future without him, a future that could support us. Us. Not him.

That's when something inside my father snapped completely. It's called an extinction burst event. It's what happens when someone who thrives on control suddenly begins to lose it. When their usual manipulations no longer produce the desired response, they don't quietly walk away. They explode. It's a psychological panic, a last-ditch effort to reassert dominance, like a drowning man pulling everyone else under with him.

That's what 1981 became: the year he began to drown. And anyone was a target for his rage, not just his own family.

He sensed the shift. My mother's new defiance. My growing resistance. The baby girl who represented hope. All of it chipped away at his reign. And the more his power slipped, the more brutal he became. His actions were no longer about anger; they were about control slipping through his fingers like sand. He went to all lengths to maintain and regain that control, like a rabid animal cornered. But something had changed. We no longer responded the way we used to. And that only made him more dangerous.

The year progressed into a blur of screaming matches, broken glass, bruises, and quiet acts of rebellion. But toward the end of the year, the tension stopped building and started cracking. Something irreversible was coming. You could feel it in the silence between screams. Like the moment before a tornado touches down.

As 1981 drew to a close, an unusual stillness settled over the house. It was quiet; not the comforting kind, but the kind that made you pause and listen harder. The chaos that usually pulsed through our walls had dimmed. For a while, there were no eruptions, no footsteps pounding overhead. Just space. And quiet.

That was the year I moved downstairs. The basement had been converted into a quasi-apartment, my own pad. At 10 years old, I had some breathing room. It wasn't far, but it was far enough. Close enough to hear the house stir but removed enough to feel like I had my own world. It became my sanctuary.

But I wasn't the only one who had staked out a space down there. Tucked behind a crude partition, near the furnace and water heater, was a cramped room that had long been my father's. It had always existed in the background as a forgotten corner of the basement. But now, it took on new life. He was always in there. Always.

He filled it with shelves of strange tools, locks, tumblers, and half-assembled devices. There was an old-fashioned printing press, rusted and obscure. Why he had brought it down there, no one knew. Locksmith gear lined the walls like trophies. And hanging from one of the ceiling rafters was a cartoonish sign showing a dazed figure on the ground beneath the words: "You want it when??" Next to it, a framed EOD (Explosive Ordinance Disposal) certificate from the U.S. government, proof of his Vietnam-era work with explosives. The combination was unnerving: part joke, part warning. And entirely real. A dark job for a dark person.

He would spend hours, days in that dark little room, tinkering, assembling, planning. I didn't know what he was doing, not really. But I knew enough to sense that something was happening in there. The peace upstairs was a byproduct of the fixation downstairs. And while the house exhaled, his mind was tightening, focusing, preparing.

The house settled into winter. The television throwing that blue light across the room. Christmas music. Familiar movies. The kind of background that comforts people.

My father chose *It's a Wonderful Life*.

I did not understand what I was seeing at first. A drugstore. A back room. Glass bottles lined like little soldiers. A pharmacist hollowed out by grief, drunk on it, trembling with it. A telegram in his hand. A mistake in his fingers. Capsules being filled for a sick child. A boy, George Bailey, watching something go wrong in real time, too young to be brave, too decent to look away.

Then the violence. The pharmacist hitting the boy. Fear turning the room sharp. George refusing to deliver the medicine and trying to explain that it contained poison, begging to be heard. The pharmacist grabbing him harder, louder, meaner, like anger could erase the error.

Then the capsule.

The pharmacist tore it open. Powder spilled out. He put it to his mouth. Tasted it. Stopped breathing for a beat. His face changed. Not anger now. Recognition. Horror. He declared. Poison.

The scene flipped. The rage collapsed into shame. The hands that struck turned unsteady. The man who almost sent death out his door broke apart. George was still a child, still shaking holding the truth like a live wire.

That is how the movie plays it. A near miss. A narrow escape. A contained catastrophe. A moral lesson wrapped in mercy.

What I remember is not the lesson.

I remember watching my father

I remember my father watching.

Not casually. Not the way people half-watch holiday movies while wrapping gifts. Not with laughter. Not with disgust. Watching with stillness. With focus. Like the screen had finally decided to speak his language.

When that capsule opened, something changed in the room. The air tightened. The house felt smaller. An eerie feeling crept over everything, slow, deliberate, intelligent. Like the walls leaned in to listen. Like the heat itself went quiet. Like the television light turned colder.

I looked at him. Waiting for a flinch. Waiting for discomfort. Waiting for any human reflex that said that is wrong.

Nothing.

Just attention.

In that moment, nobody in that house had any idea what was coming. Not my mother. Not me. Not the neighbors. Not the country. Not the victims. Nobody was thinking about tampering. About random victims. About consumer trust. About capsules as delivery systems. About poison as a choice, not an accident.

Nobody except the man in his chair.

The movie insisted poison could be caught at the threshold. A mistake corrected. A life saved. A story resolved before it could become a headline.

My life would not get that version.

In my home, poison would not be a tragic error. It would be an instrument. A method. A signature. Something practiced in silence, then released into the world with no warning, no mercy, no neat ending.

December faded. The year ran out of pages. The lights stayed up. The routines stayed intact.

But I felt it.

1982 was already there.

Not on the calendar yet, not in anyone's mouth, not in the news.

Lurking.

We called it a quiet end to the year. But it was only quiet because he had gone underground. Literally.

We were drifting closer to the event horizon. 1982 was waiting.

And it would change everything.

1982

JANUARY – THE DOOR

The new year arrived like a whisper. No celebration, no countdown, just a cold, still morning and the low creak of the basement stairs.

I remember waking up to the sound of tools. It wasn't unusual, but something about it felt different. Sharper. More deliberate. I peeked out from my bedroom door, which was a clear shot to the cramped utility corner he referred to as his workshop. He stood hunched, putting up a door frame on what had been a simple open alcove. A lair, really. The kind of place a kid's imagination turns into a dragon's cave or a secret lab. Except this wasn't imaginary. And it was changing.

He was installing a door.

Not just a door. It was a thick slab of wood with metal hinges that groaned when he tested them. He measured everything with obsessive precision. On the floor beside him was a box of new hardware: hinges, long screws, reinforced brackets.

I silently stepped back, heart pounding without reason, curiosity tugging at me. "What's the door for?" I directly asked over dinner. I was becoming braver.

He didn't look up. "Just want to keep the heat in. It's drafty down there."

My mom glanced at him but said nothing. Her silence had started growing louder by then, a silent protest that I was learning to interpret.

"But you never cared about that before," I pushed, feeling even braver.

He looked up. His eyes were tired, but there was something else festering behind them. Calculation? Caution? Guilt?

"Things change," he said flatly. "Sometimes a man needs a little space. Away from his fucking family."

A space away from his fucking family. That was what he called it. But over the coming weeks and months, the door remained shut more often than open. He began retreating behind it for hours. Sometimes, I would press my ear to the wood and hear only the hum of a light, the scrape of paper, or the low rustle of something being moved. Other times, it was dead quiet. Somehow, that was worse.

The door wasn't just a door. It was a beginning. A border. A line in the house that we weren't allowed to cross anymore.

And none of us understood, not yet, that we were already on the wrong side of it.

FEBRUARY – THE BOOK

The air in the house felt different by February. Still cold, but it wasn't just winter anymore; it was silence. Thick. Lingering. The kind that presses on your ears and makes you second-guess whether anyone's even home.

He spent most of his time behind the lair door now. The basement had become his second home, and it was rare to catch him outside of it for more than a few minutes. When he did emerge, he looked past us, like his body had returned upstairs, but his mind had stayed below.

My mom barely spoke. She moved through the house with the weariness of someone who had already said everything worth saying. At night, I could hear her pacing quietly in the kitchen. Sometimes I wondered if she wanted to leave. Or scream. Or disappear.

One Saturday, I did what seemed impossible.

I knew I shouldn't do it. I knew that, but I was growing increasingly curious. My father was gone on one of his supply runs, and that curiosity had been gnawing at me like a splinter I couldn't dig out. I crept down the basement steps, careful to skip the one that creaked, and stood before the lair door.

The door gave a slight resistance before opening. Inside, the two small windows near the ceiling barely let in any light. His workbench sat beneath a gray magnifying lamp, casting an unnatural glow over scattered tools and papers. The room smelled both damp and like something metallic had been left too close to heat.

That is when I saw the book.

It was sitting there like it belonged. Like it was a sacred text. *The Anarchist Cookbook.*

I didn't know what it was. I thought it was a recipe book at first. The title confused me; I was 10 years old. *Anarchist? Cookbook? What is an anarchist? What kind of food do anarchists eat?* The cover was plain. Black with white printing, ominous in its simplicity. I opened it, expecting pictures of food, maybe ingredients.

Instead, I saw instructions.

Diagrams. Formulas. Bombs. Poisons.

I didn't understand most of it, but I recognized words like "detonation," "ignition," and "cyanide." It felt wrong, as if I was seeing something I wasn't meant to see. Something that couldn't be unseen.

I heard the front door upstairs open and shut.

Panic flooded my body as I shoved the book back into place and darted behind the water heater. I held my breath, listening. Heavy footsteps echoed above. They stopped. Then they creaked toward the basement.

The door didn't open.

He didn't come down.

Later that night, I asked Mom, "Why does Dad have a cookbook in the workshop?"

She didn't answer at first. Then, softly, as if speaking to herself, she said, "He's always collecting strange things. You know how he is."

But I could tell from the tremble in her voice. She didn't believe that anymore.

Neither did I.

MARCH – THE LOCK

He asked me to come outside. That alone was strange.

He rarely engaged one on one unless it involved discipline or instructions. Things that didn't require emotion. But this time, he motioned to the patio bench like we were about to have a talk.

A real one.

"Sit down," he said, his voice low and measured.

I sat, my legs swinging beneath me, unsure if I was in trouble.

"We're going to be living differently for a while," he began. "Your mom and I… we're separating."

The words didn't register at first. I stared at him, blinking. My mind struggled to process it. *Separating? What does that even mean?*

He looked off toward the fence line, as if it held the answers. He looked toward a dying mulberry tree, a tree that he had killed by pounding copper nails into it. A tree that was on our neighbors' property. A tree that he used as a head on a stake to warn the world that *this could happen to you as well.*

"It's nothing to worry about. Just like when Mr. L. from church used to go on business trips, remember? This is just something I need to do. Temporary."

"What kind of business?" I asked, my voice barely audible.

He paused too long.

"Things I've been preparing for," he said finally. "It's complicated."

I didn't understand. And I could tell he wasn't going to explain further. My stomach felt hollow. I nodded anyway, because what else was I supposed to do?

A few days later, he told me that he had found an apartment nearby. He said I could see it if I wanted. I took him up on it, mostly out of curiosity. I secretly rode my bike there one afternoon. I'll never forget what it looked like. A small, peach-colored house, not far from the police station.

I peeked into the windows. Inside the house was almost empty. A mattress on the floor. A small table. A single chair. No photos. No sign of life. Just a few boxes and papers.

Back home, things were changing again. He installed something new on the lair door. I watched him do it in silence, my breath stuck in my chest.

It was a deadbolt.

Not just any kind. This one required a key on both sides to enter and to exit. "Why do you need a lock like that?" I asked, trying to sound casual.

He looked up at me. Cold eyes. Not angry. Just… unreadable again. "Some things need to stay locked up," he said, then returned to his work. He never said what those things were.

But from then on, the door never sat open again. The light under the crack disappeared entirely. If you wanted in, you needed a key.

If you wanted out, that depended on him.

APRIL – A HOUSE ON FIRE, QUIETLY

He wasn't around much. But when he was, it felt like a threat. I started to wonder if he had someone else, another family somewhere that he actually liked. Someone he could smile for. Joke with. Someone who didn't flinch when he entered the room.

When he was home, he vanished behind the locked lair door, letting the rest of the house rot around him. The yard began falling into disrepair, weeds curling up like fingers through the cracks in the concrete. Paint peeled in strips.

The house of Drozd was starting to crumble.

The foolish man built his house upon the sand...

The pressure in the house ratcheted up. The kind that distorts everything, like a heatwave on black top. His absence wasn't a relief. It made things worse, because it meant the silence had time to build. We held our breath, waiting for his return, knowing he would bring the storm.

By then, I think my mom had stopped pretending. She walked like she was moving through water. Slow, disoriented, tired in a way that sleep couldn't fix.

At Electro-Motive, where he worked full time, rumors of layoffs were spreading like wildfire. I heard him mutter under his breath one night, "They'll shut it all down. Then what?" He was never really talking to us. Just barking into the void. "Great. I'll be broke and stuck here. All. The. Time."

He didn't want to be here. That was obvious. So, he poured himself into extra shifts with the Lyons Fire Department and the Lyons Police Department. These were his side gigs. He had a passion and a pride working these jobs. He wanted to be any place but home. But even that didn't stop the escalation.

The violence came in pulses. Sudden. Unprovoked. No warning shot.

I can remember hearing the safe open in my parents' bedroom. The metal dial was spinning fast in his hands. I knew that sound. I knew what followed. Sometimes it was shouting. Other times it was worse. He would drag the gun out, cock it, and press it to my mother's temple. He would spit filth in her face like venom. "You're a fucking whore. I'm going to blow your brains out."

There were nights I would crouch on the basement steps with Justin and Liz, huddled in the dark like rats, waiting for it to be over. Waiting for the sound of a gunshot that never came but always could. Waiting for sirens. For something. Anything.

When it got bad enough, I would try to disappear with the kids. I would walk them across Joliet Avenue, AKA Route 66. A very busy stretch of highway.

I would walk them past the bar signs and the drunks in the parking lot, praying that we wouldn't be seen crossing the busy highway heading to the park. A 10-year-old with a stroller and a toddler in tow. Trying to buy time. Trying to be invisible.

That was the month I realized that I was living a life that wouldn't get better. Not for me. Not for any of us.

Yes, I had the gift of seven decent years before everything blew up. But they felt like a dream now. A fluke. Justin and Liz were too young to remember anything else. Trauma was their foundation. The bruises weren't just on our skin. They were scars that we would carry emotionally, eternally. They were in the bones of our house. In the awkward way we carried ourselves.

I remember watching them, my siblings, and wondering what would become of them if we survived this. What kind of people did this kind of life make? I stopped wondering about escape. Hope became embarrassing.

I was at an age that is difficult enough on its own. Tucked in somewhere between childhood and something else, not quite old enough to have power, but too old to be protected from the truth. That limbo is already cruel, even in the best of homes. In our home, there were no sleepovers, no birthday parties, no neighborhood kids knocking on the door asking if I could come out to play. We couldn't have friends over. Not ever. The house was much too volatile for visitors. There was too much risk that someone would hear something, see something, say something.

So, I started to pull inward. Depression and anxiety, although I didn't have names for them back then, became my closest companions. They showed up early and stayed late. At school, I tried to disappear into the edges of the classroom. At home, I mostly stayed silent. I was lonely. Sad. Angry. I would walk around with a tightness in my chest that never eased. I didn't know if I was going to cry or scream or both, but I learned how to swallow it down so no one else would notice. Because no one ever really asked. Did anyone really care?

I used to daydream that he would come back to his senses, ride in like a knight on a white horse, and make it all right. Pick my mom up in his arms like the hero in a storybook and carry us away into some kind of soft, glowing future.

But by now, that fantasy had turned rancid.

There would be no white horse. No storybook. No rescue. Only the truth.

We were living in hell.

And hell doesn't have an exit. Until...

EASTER 1982 – THE MATRIARCH MOVES IN

Unbeknownst to the residents of Gage Avenue, we were about to be invaded. A tall shadow moved in from the South. Grandma. No fanfare, no warnings. Just her commanding presence. She was a Norman, in name and in stature. Towering. Relentless. She took no shit, and she wasn't there to make friends.

"Your no-count father. Useless as tits on a tomcat," she snapped, barely through the front door. "He needs to get the hell out of the way. I'm gonna put this family back together."

Her excuse was Easter, but she lingered like a storm cloud long after the pastel eggs and stale candy were gone. I overheard her on the phone, thick Missouri accent curling every word.

"I just knew it in my bones. Mary Grace and those kids needed me. Danny is laid off, Mary Grace is a wreck, and Joey's doin' bad in school."

"There ain't no food in the freezer or pantry," she said with steel in her voice. "I'm going to put this family back together if it's the death of me."

She swore by the Church of Christ doctrine. It was gospel etched into her marrow. Acts 2:38. Repent. Be baptized. Start again. And by God, we did. She dragged us to church on Sundays, Wednesdays, whenever the doors were unlocked.

She made me memorize verses, flash cards, hymns, anything to keep my brain from rotting under the weight of the chaos.

But she also turned that church into a mirror and held it up to Danny Drozd. "You. Are. A. Hypocrite. You get dressed up and parade around that church like a Pharisee."

"I see through your bullshit. That's what it is. BULLSHIT."

"You can't fool me."

"You go and act like a decent man. Then you come home and abuse your family."

She meant every word. And for the first time ever, someone was standing up to him. I saw the sting in his eyes. It was the sting of being seen.

Grandma saw through him because she had seen it all before. He was weak, and it was showing.

She made sure he knew it.

Her brand of discipline was fierce but rooted in love. Not like the beatings I had come to expect from my father. She didn't hurt to feel power. She corrected to restore order. She saw every broken piece and tried to glue us back together.

She cleaned the yard. She stocked the pantry. She filled the fridge. She taught me the Bible, drilled my schoolwork, and reminded me constantly that I mattered. That I was worthy of love. That I wasn't invisible. That she cared.

For the first time in forever, the house smelled like food. Like safety. Like something close to peace. For a brief second, I believed we were safe again. That the ship might not sink this time.

But it never lasted, did it?

She anchored us, if only for a moment. And then she was gone. Back down to Missouri for my cousin Sherrie's high school graduation.

MAY – VERBAL CASTRATION

When Grandma delivered her now-infamous speech, the air thickened like a storm cell. H-Y-P-O-C-R-I-T-E.

That is what she called him. Loud enough for all of us to hear. Slow enough to make it sting. She spelled it out like it was carved into stone.

We all stood in that living room, frozen. No one moved. It was like witnessing a public execution, only the weapon was language, and the body didn't drop. It recoiled. I think that may have been the world's first verbal castration. She tore her son-in-law down in front of his family, stripped him of whatever false power he thought he had.

He was humiliated. Neutered. We all saw it. And oddly enough, for a brief moment, we felt safe. She called him what he was.

"Mean. Disgusting. Perverted. Violent. No-count."

Her words, not mine. But I agreed. He was a coward, a man who preyed on the vulnerable because deep down, he knew he was nothing. She forced the truth into the open like ripping off a scab. Bloody, painful, but cleansing. And for once, I could see clearly.

That was the month I began to change. I started to understand that words had teeth. That the tongue could cut deeper than a blade. I started to believe that maybe I was worthy of more.

Grandma taught me that. She taught me to fight back with grace and grit.

After her sudden departure for Sherrie's graduation, it was like a vacuum. The darkness rushed back in.

Without her presence, he inflated again. He started working out. He wore a Superman T-shirt—sometimes underneath his uniform, hidden like some warped idea of strength. Sometimes he wore it in plain view so that the world could see him coming. Except they didn't. They didn't see him coming.

He strutted around like nothing had happened. But something had. The damage was done. He was never the same. Neither were we. I can still hear my brother crying while he was beaten with that police belt.

I can't even remember what job he had then. Electro-Motive? Fire department? Police? It didn't matter. He was a fraud in every uniform, and the lies piled up like bodies. He had dreams of his peach-colored apartment, but with his layoff, that fantasy rotted before it ever materialized.

Good.

I grew bolder. Ten years old, but tall and full of fire. Grandma had planted something in me: a backbone. I started pushing back. Calling him out. He hated it. He saw me as a threat now. Not just a child to intimidate, but an obstacle. And when I stood between him and his rage, I didn't flinch.

That is around the time that I began protecting my mom. My siblings. Myself.

I remember the moment my mom looked at me differently, like maybe I could help. We were in the parking lot of Service Merchandise in Berwyn. She had picked up something, but the only thing I really remember is the look in her eyes as we sat in the car. She didn't cry. She didn't yell.

She just said, "I don't know how much more of him I can take. If he starts beating on me tonight, I need you to call the police."

I was 10. Ten.

That night, the storm broke.

I was downstairs when it happened. The air was already heavy, thick with dread. Then the thumps started. I knew that rhythm. That pattern. There was one sound I'll never forget, the unmistakable thud of a body hitting the floor. I didn't need to guess.

It was her. My mother.

She was upstairs. The kids were up there too. And I was alone below, paralyzed in the silence after the fall. I remember thinking, *How do I get to them?*

I didn't have an answer. I just remember the feeling. That helpless, crushing fear.

CHAPTER TWO: EVIL DAN

I wasn't ready to return here, not yet. Not again. But some stories don't wait for readiness. They claw their way to the surface, uninvited.

The truth is, I never actually finished the last chapter. Not really. I tried. I froze. The words stopped mid-thought, and I walked away. Maybe I told myself it was for dramatic effect. Maybe it was. Or maybe it was just that reliving those moments took more out of me than I had expected. Thoughts like those don't seek approval. They come with weight, sharp edges, and the smell of bitter almond in the air. And when I let myself go back, really go back, it started to hollow me out.

Still, this is where we left off:

Alone. In the basement.

Pounding. Screaming. Thumping. Shattering. Crying.

Fear. Darkness.

I had to do it.

I ran into the laundry room, bare feet slapping against cold linoleum. The phone was mounted on the wall. Yellow plastic, push button. A blinding orange sticker as bright as the sun next to it with the emergency numbers for the Lyons

Police and Fire Department. That was it. There was no 911 in Lyons in 1982. No shortcuts to help. Just numbers and trembling fingers.

I remember the numbers: 4.4.7.1.2.2.5.

God help you if you had an emergency and a rotary phone. No area code. No time to think. Just instinct and adrenaline. The line rang once. Twice.

Then a voice: "Lyons Police Department."

No warmth. No urgency. Just static and silence between the syllables. I forced the words out.

"I… I need help." My voice cracked in my throat, too quiet to matter.

"Hello?" the woman asked again. "I can't hear you."

I took a breath, the kind you take when you know that whatever happens next could be the beginning of the end.

"My dad. Is beating up. My mom." The words felt like broken glass in my mouth. Silence.

"Are you okay?" she asked.

"No. I mean, yes. But my mom needs help. Please."

"What's your mom's name, sweetheart?"

"Mary Drozd."

Another pause. I could hear typing. Or maybe just the beating of my heart in my ears. "Are you Danny's son?"

"Yes," I whispered. "He's hurting her. Bad."

"Hang on, sweet pea. Someone's already on their way." She didn't need the address. Everyone already knew.

This wasn't the last time I had to intervene. Each time was about the same. An officer would show up, kibbitz with my dad for a minute, and tell him, "Danny—whatever is going on in there, just knock it off."

That was it. The blue wall was real. There would be no accountability for him. Not then. Not ever. If the Lyons police had held him accountable, even once, the trajectory could have possibly been different. Maybe not. But he wouldn't have felt as untouchable. But he was. He always was. So, he continued. His violence continued. His rage continued. His plans continued.

EVIL DAN AND THE PETER PAN ILLUSION

Some people refuse to grow up. Not in a playful, harmless way, but in a way that becomes dangerous. This is referred to as the Peter Pan Syndrome, although it isn't an official diagnosis in the DSM (Diagnostic and Statistical Manual of Mental Disorders). It's when someone, often a man, avoids adult responsibilities, refuses to face consequences, and lives in a world built on fantasy, control, and denial. That was my father.

He didn't just refuse to grow up. He loathed the idea. Growing up would have meant owning up. Facing himself. Facing us. The only way he preferred to face us was with that cop belt of his. Thick and textured. That was his preferred method of punishment lately.

Instead, he created a shadow, a version of himself that he called "Evil Dan." Just like Peter Pan chased after his own shadow, my father used Evil Dan as a part of himself he could let loose, while pretending it wasn't really him. It gave him an excuse. A split. An illusion of control.

"That wasn't me. That was Evil Dan." But it was always him. Evil Dan had visited previously, but now, Evil Dan seemed to be on an extended visit.

This imaginary split gave him freedom. It allowed him to be cruel without guilt. Violent without shame. He lived in his own world, just like Peter Pan in Neverland. A place with no rules, no growing old, no accountability—except in my father's world, that fantasy came with a real-life body count.

He could say or do anything—lie, hurt, manipulate, murder—and still go to sleep at night thinking he was the hero in his own story. That is what made him dangerous. He didn't feel like the villain. He felt like the hero in his own story. He felt untouchable. Absolved because he was never culpable. It was always Evil Dan.

And just like Peter Pan needed his shadow to feel whole, my father needed Evil Dan. It gave him power. It gave him permission. But it also exposed the truth that deep down, he was afraid. Not of being caught. Not of doing harm. But of facing himself. Of being a real adult. Of ever growing up.

So, he lived as a man-child in a Superman T-shirt, proclaiming to anyone who would listen that having a badge and a gun meant that he could do whatever to whomever whenever and wherever he wanted. With no accountability, while hiding behind the name he gave his darker half. But there was no fantasy land. Just a broken house, a scared family, and a father who disappeared into the shadow he created and never came back.

CHAPTER THREE: SUMMER BREAK

JUNE 1982

It was the beginning of June. Summer was supposed to mean freedom. Sleepovers. Sprinklers. Swimming. Popsicles melting in the sun. But none of that came. Not this year. This year, it meant *him*. It meant *always*. He was always there. Watching. Hovering. A shadow that no light could seem to break through. He had been laid off from Electro-Motive. And now… *Evil Dan was here to stay.*

My mom had to run to the grocery store, or maybe she had a summer class. The specifics blur, like bad dreams tend to do. All I know is that he came home one day from the police department, still in uniform, like a twisted parody of authority. He didn't walk in. He invaded. The front door swung open with a crash that echoed down the hallway and through my bones.

He leapt over the two stairs from the foyer into the living room like a soldier storming an enemy line. I stood frozen, directly in his path. Behind me was Justin, no more than a toddler, standing in front of the playpen where Liz was napping. I instinctively stepped in front of him, my own breath shallow, protective. Justin stood wide-eyed. Paralyzed. Still.

Then, without pause, without warning, Evil Dan reached for his service weapon while still in midair. His boots hadn't even hit the ground before the gun was drawn. He had it cocked and ready. Before I could react, he was on me. He grabbed me by the shirt and jerked me into a headlock so swiftly, so violently, I could feel his breath against my temple. His nostrils flared. His eyes… they weren't human. They were something else entirely. Something predatory.

My heart pounded in my throat.

As he pressed the cold metal against my skull, he hissed the question through clenched teeth: "Do you think this gun is loaded?"

My throat tightened. My breath caught in my chest. "Yes," I choked, gasping for air. It was a scream trapped in a whisper. A scream that couldn't find its way out.

He didn't move. He didn't blink. His reply was calculated, ritualistic, drilled into me like a soldier in basic training.

"From now on, when I ask you if the gun is loaded, you answer, 'Sir, yes, sir. The gun is always loaded, sir.'"

The barrel pressed deeper. His fingers around my neck, tighter. "I am going to ask you again. Do you think this gun is loaded?"

My vision blurred as tears welled up. But I wouldn't let them fall. I had made myself a promise at a young age. Never let him see me break. Never let him see me crack.

"Sir, yes, sir. The gun is always loaded, sir."

He threw me aside. My body slammed against the floor, the edge of my skull missing our pentagon-shaped coffee table by mere inches. The near miss didn't feel like luck. It felt like a warning.

Justin was still there. In front of the playpen. Not moving.

I turned to look at him, into his eyes, and saw nothing. No spark. No emotion. He was frozen in time, like a mannequin dressed as a little boy.

Then Evil Dan turned to him. My brother. Not even four years old.

He crept forward with a terrifying calm. Shoulders squared. Posture like a hunter closing in on prey. He didn't even look at Justin. He didn't speak. He was looking me in the eyes. He simply slipped his arm around Justin as if mimicking a hug.

But the gun didn't waver. It was pressed directly to Justin's temple.

Justin couldn't speak. I knew it. His voice was gone. Fear had snatched it from him.

Evil Dan turned to me with that smirk. The same giant Cheshire Cat-like smirk I had seen before, only blacker now. His eyes weren't just black. They were hollow. His soul was even blacker.

He turned back toward me, as if savoring the moment. He was relishing our panic. "Do you think this gun is loaded?"

I straightened my spine. I met his eyes. I saw myself in their reflection, small and shaking, but I stood tall. I became still.

"Sir, yes, sir. The gun is always loaded, sir."

Behind me, Justin remained motionless. And I knew in my core, with every cell in my body, that something in him had snapped. That trauma had sealed him shut. It had frozen him. Maybe forever.

Liz began to cry. The sound sliced through the thick air like broken glass.

He walked toward her, slow and theatrical, like it was part of a show he had been rehearsing. He picked her up with one arm, as if she were just a doll, and with the other, he held the loaded and ready gun to her head.

She wasn't even one. For fuck's sake, she wasn't even a year old.

And still…

"Your little sister's life is in your hands. Now, do you think this gun is loaded?"

"Sir, yes, sir. The gun is always loaded, sir."

He placed Liz back in the playpen and walked away. Casually. As if it was nothing.

I rushed to Liz and scooped her into my arms. I held her like her life depended on it. Maybe it did. I could barely feel her through my own trembling. Her tiny body against my chest was the only thing grounding me to earth.

I turned to Justin. I called his name. Whispered. Pleaded. He didn't blink. Didn't flinch. It was 20 minutes before he even seemed to breathe again.

And to this day, *God help me,* I believe that Justin went somewhere else that day. Somewhere deep. Somewhere unreachable. And I'm not certain if all of him ever fully came back.

A few weeks after the "gun is loaded" incident, he came up with a new nickname for us. He started calling us "scrotes."

Plural. Short for scrotum.

There was no humor in it. No camaraderie. It wasn't a nickname. It was a branding, like cattle. Like property.

Like less than. He used it like a whip, snapping it through clenched teeth, forcing it into our ears until it stuck.

We didn't laugh. We didn't even flinch. We just froze. Every time.

There was something surgical in the way he said it. He knew exactly what he was doing: stripping away names, identities, childhoods. We became a crude joke in his mouth. Something to mock. Something to break.

Once he found that word, he used it relentlessly. "Get over here, scrotes."

"You little scrotes are always in the fucking way."

"Shut the fuck up, scrotes."

And we did. We got over there. We moved out of the way. We shut the fuck up. He didn't need a gun to do damage. He just needed the right word.

This was psychological warfare.

JULY 1982 – PSYCHOLOGICAL WARFARE
SATURDAY, JULY 3, 1982

There were coupons on the kitchen countertop. My mom must have left them there. Remnants from Last Sunday's *Chicago Tribune*. On top of the stack was a coupon for a free bottle of new Children's Chewable CoTylenol. McNeil Consumer Products had started a heavy advertising campaign for their new product.

Evil Dan was enraged. He took the stack of coupons and viciously tore them up and threw them into a bin to burn tomorrow.

"These fuckers are going to kill a kid. Motherfuckers." He was losing it.

SUNDAY, JULY 4, 1982

The month didn't just start off with a bang. It detonated.

Every Fourth of July up until I was eight or so had been filled with small-town tradition and innocent celebration. The parade in Lyons was a highlight, and I would walk alongside my dad in his fireman's uniform, clutching his gloved hand and feeling like a hero's child. But July 1982 stood in a different realm altogether. That summer, something far more insidious than fireworks was taking shape.

Things were unrecognizably dark now. Sad. Sickly. There was a dryness in my throat I couldn't quench, a constant dread in the pit of my stomach. Loneliness clung to me like the humidity in the air. I began to feel like a ghost in my own house, present but untethered. The firecrackers, the Roman candles, the screeching bottle rockets—those were no longer just for show. They were rituals. They were expressions. They were explosions of something internal. Both Dan and Evil Dan reveled in them.

Fireworks weren't just entertainment. They were power. Control. A momentary escape from the mundane. We had them in excess. Store-bought and homemade, they became the focal point of the month. In the front yard, we played to the crowd. In the back yard, we played to our demons.

He would bury M-80s, firecrackers equal in strength to a quarter stick of dynamite, into the dirt like landmines in the back yard. He watched with glee as they left open craters in the earth, each blast a small victory. I watched too, still only 10 years old, eyes wide and pulse racing. My mind knew better, but my body didn't. The chaos fed my fear and fascination in equal parts.

I watched him that month with the cautious curiosity of someone studying a predator. He had found a new obsession. It involved a strange gray powder. Chemical, sour. He would tear small sheets of aluminum foil and carefully spoon the powder into the center, like he was wrapping candy. When he placed it on the ground, a sudden hiss erupted.

HISSSSSSSS.

And then came the smoke. Acrid. Pungent. The stench of sulfur and eggs and something else, like something dead.

He grinned and stepped back, like a magician revealing a trick.

"Watch that," he whispered, like he was letting me in on something sacred.

What he was letting loose was a chemical reaction that he had learned in one of his favorite texts: *The Poor Man's James Bond.* This is a compilation of paramilitary knowledge and homebrewed anarchy. The formula was crude but effective. Hydrochloric acid, often in the form of muriatic acid[2], could be purchased from hardware stores. He always had a ready supply for our pool.

---

2. THE HYDROCHLORIC ACID GOODY: The hydrochloric acid goody is the most fun in the whole book. It takes many forms and works on the principle that hydrochloric acid reacts with aluminum powder, foil or metal, releasing a great, dark cloud of noxious gas which looks horrible and smells worse. Hydrochloric acid is used for killing algae in swimming pools and for cleaning tile and stone work.

Where swimming pools are common it can be bought at the supermarket for less than a dollar a gallon. It is also sold at hardware stores. Being only 37% strength, it is seldom harmful to the skin but will eat through clothing like battery acid. Hydrochloric acid is also known as muriatic acid. On damp nights, a bottle of the acid alone, broken in the midst of a crowd, will form noxious clouds of chlorine gas. Scream "Poison gas!" and you will have a panic that will give you laughs for years. (*The Poor Man's James Bond.* Vol. 1. pp. 19-20.)

Muriatic acid could be combined with certain metals, aluminum being a common one, to create hydrogen chloride gas. When released in even small amounts, it formed dark clouds that looked harmless but were, in fact, lethal. Breathing it in could scar the lungs, burn the throat, and, in high enough concentrations, suffocate you.

I didn't understand the full chemistry at the time. I just knew it was dangerous. I knew because of the way he stared at the smoke. Not like it was a toy, but like it was a weapon. Something to be respected. Something to be feared.

And he loved fear.

I couldn't explain what was happening. Not in words that made sense. The backyard playground that he had built for me was gone, replaced by the thunderclap of explosives and the sickening hiss of chemical gas.

I remember that Fourth of July evening vividly. He lit a fire in our backyard fireplace with old documents from his lair. The stack of coupons from the kitchen. Handwritten papers filled with drawings, schematics, and handwritten chemical equations. He claimed they were trash. But I saw them and how carefully he chose each one. How he paused just slightly before feeding them to the flames.

We stood silently, watching them burn.

"I could clear a building with that smoke," he muttered, nodding to his foil magic trick. "No one would even know what hit 'em."

He wasn't joking.

In retrospect, I believe the July fireworks were a cover, a noise to mask the real test runs. These chemical experiments and formulations weren't just playtime. They were rehearsals.

Preparations for something more. What? I didn't know yet.

While everyone else looked to the sky that summer, cheering the bursts of red, white, and blue, I watched the ground. I watched him. Every move, every glance. Because the war wasn't overseas. It wasn't in the news. It had taken up residence in our back yard and in our home. It was psychological.

Poisons offer a quiet alternative to things that go *boom* in the night…

SUNDAY, JULY 18, 1982 – BIRTHDAY PARTY

July didn't stop for anyone. Liz turned one on July 15. A milestone. Her first birthday. And just two days later, on July 17, I turned 11, a number that felt big at the time. Awkward, in between. Not quite a child, not yet a teenager. Old enough to feel everything deeply. Young enough to still hope birthdays meant something.

What should have been a day of celebration became a muted formality. A birthday party. A strained performance in the theater of dread. A few family members showed up, either unaware or willfully ignoring the thick unease that had settled in our house.

The birthday cakes came from Weber's Bakery. Liz's was topped in a pink spray, mine in blue. Both had matching edible flowers. Artificially bright, unnaturally cheerful. I remember staring at those flowers longer than I should have, hypnotized by the way they sat atop the sugary icing like nothing was wrong.

Eating those cakes at that time felt like eating a lie, a confectionery mask over something no one wanted to confront. The cakes should have been about growth, about life, about marking time with happiness. They felt more like a distraction. Like a decoy. Pastel-covered silence.

And then someone, I don't remember who, mentioned the name of the cake. "It's a strawberry bomb cake," they said, half-laughing.

A bomb cake. Even the cake couldn't escape the theme and the irony of this month. I glanced at my dad. He grinned at the name. He always seemed to find symbolism where others saw coincidence.

As July limped toward its end, I felt the shadows lengthen, both outside and within. The fireworks had stopped, but the residue lingered. In our yard. In my lungs. In my memory. The laughter had gone quiet. The house had retreated even more inward.

TUESDAY, JULY 27, 1982 – GRANNIE'S BIRTHDAY

We marked Grannie's birthday in style, which in our house meant Weber's Bakery and chlorine in the summertime. The bakery knew us by name every July.

It was around 89 degrees with a little rain, but nothing that could stop Grannie. She cannonballed into our four-foot-high above-ground pool like she was heading for cannonball Olympic gold.

She wore her one-piece black suit with full confidence, carrying the aura of Esther Williams in our Lyons back yard.

I had to run into the poolroom to grab a floating chair to relax and enjoy the sunshine with Grannie. Our *poolroom,* as we called it, was a storage area connected to the outside by a door and three stairs. You could enter the basement through a separate, inner door. We stored all of our pool toys, chemicals, hoses, etc. in that room. Including Evil Dan's supply of muriatic acid.

On the wall was an old cabinet. Old plywood painted turd brown. No matter what or when, you could open that turd brown cabinet and see a spider or 10. I hated that cabinet. I had to go into the cabinet to get the air pump. As I reached in to get the pump, I was hoping that a spider or a thousand-legger wouldn't fall out on me. As I pulled out the air pump, I heard a thump hit the floor.

I looked down and I saw an old manual. It was more than a pamphlet, but not quite a book. I squinted in the darkness to see what it was as I reached down to pick it up. On the cover were the words *How To Kill.* How to kill what? Spiders and thousand-leggers? I was down for that. Bugs in the pool? Okay with that too. I put it back in the turd brown cabinet with the spiders and thousand-leggers and ran back out to have fun in the pool with Grannie. I was a kid. I didn't know what that manual would turn out to be.

I ran back to the pool and stood on the deck of the pool, backward. I was going to do a TikTok of our era. No, there was no TikTok in 1982. I stood still and let my body fall backward into the pool. We called it the Nestea Plunge. It was all the rage then, every summer. We didn't have much to do back then.

Grannie applauded my Nestea Plunge and continued splashing around. Then physics took over. Out of Grannie's bathing suit popped two rogue passengers. Not quite flotation devices, but close enough. They bobbed toward the filter like rubber duckies on holiday. Imagine two chicken cutlets adrift, carried gently by the current. That is the image burned into my memory. A pool party suddenly sponsored by Tyson.

We all laughed. Grannie didn't care. She swam on like nothing had happened.

"Uh oh. Who gives a shit?" She laughed and kept splashing around the pool.

Dan, of course, was nowhere to be found. He hated his mother too much for birthdays. In fact, he hated just about everything that smacked of normal human attachment. A pool full of runaway pasties floating like party favors was probably too much joy and laughter for him to handle.

WEDNESDAY, JULY 28, 1982 – OH YEAH. WHERE IS DAN?

I hadn't seen him since before Grannie's birthday. Then, without warning, he appeared early this morning. He strode into the house in his police uniform. He carried himself like he always did: shoulders squared, arrogance hanging off him like a second skin. His Superman T-shirt, no doubt beneath the badge and fabric, was a private reminder to himself that he was untouchable.

But my eyes caught what his swagger tried to hide. Across the front of his shirt, on the sleeves too, blotches of color clung stubbornly to the fabric. Brownish-red stains, smeared like old rust, like dried earth after rain. My stomach tightened. He saw me looking. His face shifted, sharp and alert, predator to prey in a split second.

Then he vanished into the bathroom, slamming the door behind him. Moments later, he came out carrying the uniform in a bundle, rushed past me, and headed for the basement. What froze me wasn't the stains themselves but what came next. Dan put the uniform into the washing machine. Himself.

In all my life, I had never once seen him touch that machine. He treated it like it belonged to another world. One beneath him. Yet there he stood. Fumbling with the dials. Forcing the machine to swallow his uniform whole.

The sound of the washer filled the house, a mechanical heartbeat pulsing over silence. I stood there, my own heart pounding in rhythm with the spin. I know what I saw. I know what he wanted to erase.

What were those stains?

AUGUST 1982 – LIONS, AND TIGERS, AND KOOL-AID. OH MY.

August in the Midwest is a cruel trick. The sun still beats down like July, but the wind whispers otherwise. There is a noticeable shift, and you feel it in your bones. The light slants just a little differently. The cicadas chatter louder, and the air carries that unmistakable scent of dying grass and overripe tomatoes. A foreshadowing.

As August began, he had a new term of endearment for us. "Slaves." That is what he was calling us then. He would burst through the front door, arms outstretched in theatrical delight, exclaiming, "I'm so glad my slaves are here waiting to serve me!" He insisted we refer to him as "Kind Sir," as if the name might somehow mask the cruelty underneath. He was a twisted fucker.

We started making regular trips out to the city of Warrenville. Probably twice a month, sometimes more.

Warrenville was a quiet little hamlet far from the chaos that seemed to hover permanently over Gage Avenue. I cannot remember now who ended up there first. Maybe it was Randy and Mary (Dan's brother and sister-in-law), or maybe it was Mary Ann and Jimmy (longtime friends). It didn't matter much. Eventually, they were all out there.

He loved going out to Warrenville, diving headfirst into whatever project they had going on. He helped Randy and Mary fix up their house, always eager to be involved. He threw himself into helping Mary Ann and Jimmy work on the electrical circuit in their attic/loft. Meanwhile, our own house slowly started falling apart. Again. Piece by piece. Project by ignored project.

We were still in summer. But that smell was the end of summer/beginning of fall.

I can sit here while writing, and I can still smell those smells. The fresh cut grass. Charcoal in the grill. Bug repellent and Coppertone. How the scent of the grass changed as the color of the grass changed from green to yellow to brown.

This is the time when my parents decided we needed to act like a family. Or at least pretend. I don't remember any dramatic announcement. There was no sit-down moment of reconciliation.

Just an unspoken truce, the kind born not from forgiveness but fatigue. Everyone was tired of fighting. So, they made a decision: Let's take a trip. Let's look normal.

Our first attempt? The Milwaukee Zoo. Our last attempt? The Milwaukee Zoo.

I was acquiring an education in irony. This irony wasn't lost on me. A zoo. Trapped animals on display, pacing cages, pretending not to mind. The trip itself was brutal. We loaded up into our 1981 silver Buick Century station wagon and headed north. I still remember how the blue vinyl seats burned the backs of my legs. How the air conditioning sputtered, then died somewhere around Racine.

No one spoke. Not really. Just a quiet, pulsing tension. Justin fussed. Liz squirmed. I kept my eyes out the window. My parents didn't argue. They didn't even exchange glances. That silence was worse than yelling. It meant something had solidified.

Evil Dan… he was there too. Not just in the car. In him. That look in his eye, the way his fingers twitched like they were waiting for a reason. Every so often, one of us would break the silence. A sneeze. A whimper. A baby's cry. That was enough. He would swing his hand back without turning his head, like a snake striking in reverse. It didn't matter who it landed on. He just needed to strike.

Once, Liz let out a tiny cry. Not a scream. Just one of those soft, confused sounds babies make. And before anyone could comfort her, his hand snapped through the air. My mom flinched even though he didn't hit her. I remember that flinch more than the slap.

When we finally got to the zoo, this was supposed to be the fun part. The reward. The normalcy.

But the day dragged on. I remember the smell of hot asphalt mixed with animal shit. The lion exhibit looked like a war zone. Flies, heat, pacing, frustration. I watched one tiger stare at the fence, not the people. Like it was trying to remember how it ever got there in the first place.

I could relate.

We walked the loop through the zoo. We smiled for strangers, for the illusion. Evil Dan put his arm around my mom for exactly one picture and dropped it the second the shutter clicked.

Everything was an act. Every gesture was a scene in a play we hadn't auditioned for.

We left before sunset. The car ride home was just as quiet, just as long. Except now, the air felt heavier. The illusion had failed. We weren't a family.

I have been to many places in my life since then. States, countries, and cities that brought me anxiety, fear, or dread for different reasons. But I have never had a memory like that one. I have never felt more trapped than I did that day in Milwaukee. It wasn't just the car. Or the zoo. Or the heat.

It was the knowing.

Knowing that this was what trying looked like. And we had failed.

AUGUST CONTINUED – CREEPY SCIENCE STORE

We were now approaching the end of August. Summer was officially winding down. I was mentally preparing to go back to school. Not in a negative, but in a positive way. I can honestly say that August of 1982 was the longest month of my life. The summer of 1982 would officially go down as the worst summer of my life. Likewise, the year 1982 would go down as the worst year of my life.

Before August would let me go and move forward with my life, we had one more adventure to go on. It's safe to say that we had full custody of Hyper Dan at this point. His friends,

Regular Dan and Evil Dan, were stopping in for visits quite regularly. But Hyper Dan's appearance today in particular was duly noted.

He was up early and went to bed late. Run, run, run.

Go, go, go.

Today, he had an outing planned for just the two of us: Creepy Science Store.

We got into the station wagon. We started out early, and it was chilly. Good thing we had gotten through most of the hot days that August had to offer that year.

As we headed down Ogden Avenue, he popped a cassette into the player in the car. It was possible to make your own mix tape. I don't know if that is what he had done because the music on this tape was, well, out of the ordinary. He put the tape in, turned up the volume, and I shit you not. These are the words I heard:

Spring is here, a-suh-puh-ring is here
Life is skittles and life is beer
I think the loveliest time of the year is the spring
I do, don't you? (Course you do)
But there's one thing that makes spring complete for me
And makes every Sunday a treat for me

All the world seems in tune on a spring afternoon
When we're poisoning pigeons in the park
Every Sunday you'll see my sweetheart and me
As we poison the pigeons in the park
When they see us coming
The birdies all try an' hide
But they still go for peanuts
When coated with cyanide
The sun's shining bright

Everything seems all right
When we're poisoning pigeons in the park

We've gained notoriety
And caused much anxiety
In the Audubon Society
With our games
They call it impiety
And lack of propriety
And quite a variety
Of unpleasant names
But it's not against any religion
To want to dispose of a pigeon

So if Sunday you're free
Why don't you come with me
And we'll poison the pigeons in the park
And maybe we'll do
In a squirrel or two
While we're poisoning pigeons in the park

We'll murder them all
Amid laughter and merriment
Except for the few
We take home to experiment
My pulse will be quickenin'
With each drop of strych'nine
We feed to a pigeon
It just takes a smidgin!
To poison a pigeon in the park.

—Tom Lehrer "Poisoning Pigeons in the Park"

This man was fucking insane. He laughed hysterically as we drove down Ogden Avenue.

"How'd you like that one?"

I had no words. I didn't want to know what was up next on his macabre-insane-mother-fucking-crazy-ass-fucked-up-deranged mixtape.

Dan had taken me to Creepy Science Store a few times previously. Our established and well-traveled route to Creepy Science Store was Ogden Avenue to First Avenue. Hang a right. Travel through Brookfield, Maywood...

Wait... what are we doing now? He had the Beach Boys blaring "Help Me Rhonda." He turned off of First Avenue. We turned right onto what looked like a gravel parking area. Nothing attached to it, just a small turn onto gravel near the woods.

This was a section of First Avenue where the road curves. There was a guardrail that looked like it had seen an accident or two in its day. He walked with me over from the gravel parking area to a grassy area. To this day, I can still smell that fall smell in the air, especially after the hot days we'd had. The grass was tall and brown.

My father stood there and proclaimed to me, "I've noticed that you have been very observant lately. Almost, maybe, possibly... too observant."

Oh fuck, I thought. *He brought me here to kill me.*

He proceeded to walk me over to the grass area closest to the crumpled guardrail. I just knew this was it for me. He was in some type of hyper/manic mode, and it was getting really scary.

I stood my ground. Ready to fight or flee, but absolutely not freeze. I was ready to take him on. He started to tell me a story. I don't know if there was any truth to it.

"There was a pretty bad accident here recently," he started. "Let's see just how observant you really are. Use your powers of observation and look for any evidence of a car accident. Anything that you think may have been from an accident."

I didn't feel completely safe, but I trampled through the tall grass. Searching. Looking. For anything.

Right off the bat, I found a few broken pieces of glass. Some looked like broken bottles. Others looked like they could have been from a car. I showed him, and he said,

"That's easy. Any moron could find those. Search harder."

I stayed calm and continued searching. I found a few crumpled pieces of metal.

"No. Not good enough. You need to find some evidence for me. Real evidence. Not just some shit laying on the side of the road."

I searched deeper and deeper into the grasses. Something glinted ever so quickly in the sunlight. I dove down to retrieve it. I was sort of beneath the grass at this time, on my hands and knees, retrieving whatever it was.

I found it. I grabbed it. I held it. I looked, and I saw that it was a watch. Not just any watch. The watch was a khaki green Timex. I don't remember if the strap was fully attached or not. It appeared as if it had been ripped from an unknown arm. The lens was cracked, and it wasn't running. In the whole 30 seconds I had that watch, I did a full visual inspection.

Khaki green. Timex. Maybe a man's watch. Maybe a woman's. Strap possibly not fully attached. Not running. Cracked lens. Was it not working due to the obvious damage, or was it because, at this point in time, many watches were manual wind, and this watch needed to be wound? More questions than answers. Not a bad analysis for an 11-year-old in 30 seconds.

I stood up with my find. Hyper Dan stood still for a moment. The moment he stood still was longer than the amount of time that I had the watch in my possession.

"I can't fucking believe you found that." He sighed. "Good job."

It was at this point that he grabbed the watch from my hand. He placed it in his right pants pocket and gave me his typical admonition. "Do. Not. Tell. Your mother. About this."

I was asking in my head, *Is this it? He brought me here to find a broken watch?*

Something changed in his demeanor as we walked back to the car. I felt, in some sick and disgusting way, that we had bonded. Almost as if he respected me.

We got in the car and headed back down First Avenue. As soon as we got through Maywood, past the police and the court buildings, he reached into the back seat. He reached back and grabbed his blue light that was for fire emergencies only. He plugged the blue light into the cigarette lighter, rolled his window down, and, with the magnet on the underside of the blue light, he plopped it on the roof of the station wagon.

He put the pedal to the metal, and we FLEW down First Avenue. Now, he had the windows fully down, blue light flashing, and blasting the Beach Boys' "Little Deuce Coupe."

Once again, I shit you not.

I was exhausted, both mentally and physically, and we hadn't even gotten to Creepy Science Store yet. And with the way he was driving, I wasn't sure that we would.

WE MADE IT

By the time we pulled up to 5700 Northwest Highway, he had taken the blue light off the roof of the car and had the windows rolled up. Creepy Science Store was/is an actual place. Officially, its name is American Science & Surplus. They have since moved out of the Northwest Highway location.

He opened my car door for me and ushered me into AS&S like I was the Godfather. This is true. For the next few weeks, he treated me like a Don.

We entered the store, and I was standing at eye level with jar upon jar of frogs in jars. I stared with both amazement and terror. They were suspended in liquid.

Formaldehyde, to be exact. Frozen in time. Legs out wide as if caught in a memory of their previous life. Eyes open wide to blankly stare back at me.

I had no time to lament over the frogs today. My personal mission was to see what he was doing and saying. Most importantly, what he bought.

I found him walking down an aisle. I stalked him in the store. "Move stealthily and quietly so your prey will not know you're stalking them." His words. Not mine.

I watched him. He picked up something small and metallic. Not very big at all. It had an arm on the side of it. Like a lever.

Next on his shopping list was something round. The only way I can describe it is that it looked just like a rotary phone dial. Small and clear plastic. What the fuck was that?

I have spent my life since that day wondering what that round thing was. I was fortunate/unfortunate enough to find out while doing research for this book.

That was it. We drove all this way for a broken watch and some weird—very weird—items. We headed back to Lyons, going the reverse direction that we came.

SECTION TWO

CHAPTER FOUR: SEPTEMBER 1-24, 1982

INTRODUCTION

When I began working on this book, I had one mission in mind: to tell the truth. The truth about my life, my journey, and the deeply dark man at the center of my life.

I have mentioned my father's reading material, which he kept under lock and key in his lair. I have mentioned three titles that he kept in his personal library. Listed below are the three titles with a brief explanation of each.

These aren't run-of-the-mill books that you would find at your run-of-the-mill bookstore. No. These are books and articles that you would need to search out. These books and articles would be the 1980s equivalent of the dark web.

These three works stand as the most notorious examples of instruction manuals that cross the boundary between provocative political dissent or survival tactics and genuine criminal facilitation. Each of the books were kept in my father's lair and each continues to raise questions about censorship, responsibility, and the boundaries of free speech.

THE ANARCHIST COOKBOOK

Written in 1969 and published in January 1971 by 19-year-old William Powell, *The Anarchist Cookbook* compiled instructions for building explosives, creating illicit drugs, manufacturing improvised weapons, booby traps, tear gas, phreaking devices, and more, aiming to spur revolutionary action in the context of growing distrust in the U.S. government and opposition to the Vietnam War.

The FBI described the book as one of the "crudest, low-brow, paranoid writing efforts." Although the FBI concluded that the text was protected under the First Amendment, it didn't legally incite forcible resistance. The FBI did, however, retain records on the book and monitor its spread. Over the years, it has been linked to several real-world violent events, including bombings, shootings, and extremist plots, highlighting its troubling influence on violent individuals.

The book remains one of the most controversial publications of modern times. It's still widely circulated online despite its age. Critics, including anarchists themselves, have condemned it as irresponsible.

THE POOR MAN'S JAMES BOND

Authored by survivalist Kurt Saxon (born Donald Eugene Sisco, 1932–2021), *The Poor Man's James Bond* is a series of do-it-yourself guidebooks. They were first published in the early 1970s, detailing improvised weapons, booby-traps, poisons, munitions, and homemade defense tools. Saxon was a prolific survivalist writer and is credited with coining the term "survivalist."

The book was self-published and described by law enforcement as dangerous. Saxon produced multiple volumes and updated editions through the years, including Volume I, Volume II, and revised editions into the 1990s. One of Saxon's ideas was advising his readers to add poison to medication capsules as early as 1972.

HOW TO KILL

Written by John Minnery and published by Paladin Press in 1973, the book title tells it all.

Minnery favors cyanide or strychnine and suggests poisoning food, drinks, saltshakers, or sugar bowls. He recommends adding sulfuric or muriatic acid to mouthwash, eyedrops, or eardrops and adding powdered glass to the water in an ice cube tray before freezing it.

"With poisons, always give the double amount necessary to kill; this will ensure that there is no chance of survival."

"When used properly, poisons can be one of the most effective weapons in an assassin's armory. They're to be used in situations requiring quiet, rapid death."

SEPTEMBER 1, 1982

September 1982 arrived with a strange and sticky heat in Lyons, Illinois. On September 1, the temperature reached a humid 86 degrees, highly unusual for that time of year. A bit of rain fell, but even the storms felt confused, as if they, too, didn't know how to behave. The air outside was thick. The temperature in September fluctuated both inside and outside the house.

I was still on summer break, clinging to those last fragile days before school resumed after Labor Day. I should have been anxious about sixth grade, but strangely enough, I wasn't. After the hell that was that summer, school actually seemed like a vacation. Predictable. Structured. Safe.

And yet something felt off. Dan was in a good mood—and that was far more unsettling than if he had been stomping around or slamming doors.

He was… giddy.

Not giddy like a proud dad, or someone who had just gotten a raise. Giddy like a sixth-grade schoolgirl. Buzzing. Manic. He couldn't sit still. He would hum or whistle to himself. He would chuckle at things no one else found funny. In fact, he would laugh at things with no explanation, as if he were having a hilarious conversation in his own head. You never really knew.

And the worst part was that he wanted company. Hyper Dan didn't want to be alone. He didn't want to stew in his lair or hide in the shadows like Evil Dan. No, this version wanted to go somewhere, anywhere, nearly all of the time. He wanted us to match his pace, catch his current, ride his wave. He would burst into a room full of energy, demanding attention, demanding motion, demanding reaction.

Looking back, I don't know which version of him was worse. With Evil Dan, you could at least see the storm clouds. You could brace yourself. Avoid him. Get out of the way. But Hyper Dan?

There was no shelter from that.

He would wake up early and hit the ground running. He would head out to McCook for work when not laid off. He would come home to change, sometimes multiple times a day, then dash off to either the Lyons Police Department or the Fire Department, depending on his shift. He acted like he was saving the world, but he wouldn't tell us what exactly he was doing. It was all grand gestures, vague talk, and cryptic little grins.

SEPTEMBER 2, 1982

Something had shifted. His mood was still revved, but the sparkle was gone, replaced by a new edge. Not rage. Not euphoria. Precision. He was quiet, calculating. A man who was narrowing his focus. A man closing in on something unknown.

He came home with something that day. A surprise. And he couldn't wait to show it to us.

From the pocket of his red Lyons Fire Department jacket, he pulled two cups: a whitish plastic cup and a pink plastic cup. They were Tupperware midget cups.

Midget cups held two ounces and were made of polypropylene.[3] We had quite a few of these, along with other Tupperware items in our home. They were designed to hold salad dressing or sugar. My grandma had been an all-star Tupperware salesperson previously.

Slowly, as if doing a magic trick, he put the pink cup back into the other pocket of his red jacket. As if I didn't notice that.

---

3. Polypropylene, the material from which Tupperware midget cups are manufactured, is recognized for its exceptional chemical resistance and durability. When storing hazardous compounds such as cyanide and mercury, an airtight container is essential to prevent exposure to air and moisture, which can degrade the compounds or release dangerous vapors. Polypropylene's non-reactive nature and impermeability to moisture make it one of the most suitable materials for such storage.

"Mercury," he said, reverent. His voice dropped like he was revealing scripture.

He popped the lid off slowly, like he wanted to savor the moment. Inside was the mercury. Thick, sluggish, silvery. It looked like molten metal had come to life. He poured the contents onto our beige linoleum floor.

It rolled like it had a mind of its own. Beads scattered and then merged together again. The surface tension of watching the mercury was hypnotic. It didn't behave like anything I had ever seen. It didn't belong here.

"It's heavy," he whispered. "Really heavy. You wouldn't believe it until you hold it. It's safe to pick it up."

So, Justin and I both picked up the mercury and continued to play with it for a few minutes.

This wasn't a science lesson. Anyone with the title "Dr." in their name could tell you that this stuff is highly toxic.

This was theater. And the mercury wasn't the star of the show. He was.

What I remember more than the mercury was that I couldn't stop thinking about the pink cup.

I saw it. Identical in size and shape. Sealed just as tightly. But he never opened that one. Never mentioned what was inside. He didn't even acknowledge that he had it. He hid it.

He knew I had seen it, and he smiled. Not with his mouth, but with his eyes. That Cheshire-Cat grin. That knowing, smug glint that meant he had plans. That he was already 10 steps ahead of me. Of everyone.

The mercury was dangerous. I had that feeling instantly. But the pink cup? The pink cup was a mystery.

A mystery I was determined to solve.

That night I lay awake thinking about both of them, the white cup and the pink cup. Death by mercury poisoning from the whitish cup. Was there death in the pink cup as well? I didn't know yet what was coming, but I knew something was off. Way off.

Because in Dan's world, danger was just another word for fun surprise.

"The Militant, wanting a lethal supply of chemicals without giving a clue as to what he wants them for, arranges his orders somewhat like this:

ORDER ONE

1 lb. dextrin
1 lb. potassium nitrate
1 lb. sodium fluoride
1 lb. sulfuric acid
1 lb. potassium ferrocyanide
1 lb. barium peroxide
1 lb. iron filings

ORDER TWO

1 lb. iron oxide, red
¼ lb. sodium (metallic)
¼ Ib. red phosphorous
¼ lb. potassium permanganate
2 oz. powdered magnesium
1 lb. potassium carbonate

ORDER THREE

1 lb. calcium chloride
1 lb. potassium chlorate
2 oz. potassium cyanide

1 lb. sodium peroxide
1 lb. powdered charcoal
1 lb. aluminum powder (paint grade)
1 lb. calcium oxide
1 lb. black antimony sulphide"

(*The Poor Man's James Bond* Vol.1. pp. 14-15)

FRIDAY, SEPTEMBER 3, 1982

First day back at school. This was School District 103's annual half day back before Labor Day. Why did we go for a half day and then have a long holiday weekend? Who can say?

The kids at school laughed, shoved, and moved on with their lives. No one else had mercury in their house. No one else had Evil Dan waiting in the basement. No one else had to tiptoe through a minefield just to make it to dinner alive.

The second I got home, I could already hear him below. In the lair.

I didn't know what he was doing down there, but I knew it involved the pink midget cup. Something lived in that pink cup.

I had thought about that pink cup the night before. The silence around it was heavier than the mercury inside the whitish one. It haunted me at school. I needed to know.

So, I did it.

I walked to the edge of the stairs and went to the basement. Very carefully, like I was stepping into a war zone.

He appeared in the doorway of the lair without a sound. I asked. Quietly. Bravely.

"What's in the pink cup?"

He stared at me for a long time. Not angry. Calculating. Amused that I had the balls to ask. "You don't need to know," he said flatly.

But I didn't back down. I pressed. Just enough.

He leaned in, lowering his voice like he was sharing a nuclear secret. "If you really want to know…" A long pause. "It's kryptonite."

He locked eyes with me.

"Do. Not. Ever. Touch. That pink cup. EVER!"

"But…" I said, still halfway in childhood logic. **"I thought kryptonite only killed Superman."**

He smiled. Slowly. Eyes dead.

"That's what most people think. But no. Kryptonite can kill anyone. **Anyone."**

The silence after that sentence could have drowned me.

I didn't want to know any more. Except I did. Whatever was in that pink cup wasn't meant to be known. Not by me. Maybe not by anyone.

That was enough for one day.

I didn't want to upset Evil Dan.

I retreated to my room, shut the door, and planned my trespass into the lair.

SATURDAY, SEPTEMBER 4, 1982

The previous night, I had waited intently for him to exit the lair. I watched him through the crack in my bedroom door. I watched him take his keys off his belt loop and fish around for the key. Why did this man have so many fucking keys? I was watching to see which key locked his magical lair.

I saw it. It was strategically placed a few keys in from the end. It was a Schlage key. I knew it was a Schlage because of all the locksmithing jobs I had gone on with him previously. Yes, it was the Schlage key very near the end.

A disdain was developing for this man.

I had always hoped that things would get better. I knew they weren't, though, so I was learning to adapt. I was learning how to read him. I was watching him to understand him. My education in psychopathy was just beginning.

When opportunity knocks, you answer the door. And opportunity knocked that Saturday.

He and my mom had gone somewhere. Where? I didn't know. I didn't care. They were out of the house, and bonus—Justin and Liz were with them, and they. Took. My mom's. Keys.

Yes. His keys were left on the hook next to the glass block window in the foyer.

I marched upstairs, grabbed those keys, and took a clear mental picture of exactly how they had been placed. He was training me well. Details mattered.

Back downstairs. I stood at the lair door, heart pounding. Hands shaking. I was going in. I found the Schlage key and inserted the key into the lock.

Bingo. It fit. This was the key. I turned the lock. I was waiting for an alarm to go off, perhaps a spring gun pointed at the door. But nothing. I reached to my left and turned on the light. The sound of the overhead fluorescents buzzed.

BUZZZZZZZZZ.

I took a quick look around the lair. What a mess. He was a hoarder, and this room proved it. I crept in very quietly, making sure to look up and down—just like he taught me. *"Move silently when you're stalking,"* I could hear him say.

I don't believe that he would have ever thought I would use his lessons in psychopathy against him.

I didn't want to make any sudden moves, but I knew I had a limited time for this mission. I scanned the room. A few bullet trays, the gray magnifying light, hordes of papers. Oh yes, we cannot forget *The Anarchist Cookbook*. It was still present and accounted for.

Where was that fucking cup? There was a small area to the left of the door when you walked in. Almost like an alcove. That alcove butted up against the bathroom, which was on the other side of the wall.

This is new, I thought.

He had built a crude countertop placed upon sawhorses. About two feet above that, there were wooden shelves. Three of them, to be exact. Placed horizontally, one above the other, with about a foot in between each.

I froze for a moment. My mind was playing tricks on me. I would have sworn that I heard the front door open. False alarm. I thoroughly scanned those shelves. On the middle of the three shelves, I could barely see them peeking out from behind a stack of paper—the lids from the two midget cups.

There they were. I very carefully pulled up his stool after memorizing its exact placement on the other side of the lair. I placed the stool in front of the countertop. I climbed up onto the stool.

As I climbed onto the stool, on the lowest shelf, I saw stacks of papers. *How to Kill* was one of them.

That manual was in the turd brown cabinet in the poolroom at Grannie's birthday party.

I didn't have time to inspect the manual. I was on a mission.

I had eyes on the cups. The cup closest to me was the whitish one with the mercury. Next to it was the pink one. The stack of papers they were hidden behind was titled, *The Poor Man's James Bond.*

What's this now? A script for some deranged play?

I moved the cup of mercury over, and I reached for the pink cup. The verboten pink cup. There was nothing standing between us now.

I had the pink cup in my hand and noted that there appeared to be powder in the cup. That powder filled the cup nearly three quarters of the way to the top.

I froze.

ABORT. ABORT.

What do you expect? I was 11 years old.

I made sure everything was back in place and locked the lair back up with the Schlage key.

SUNDAY, SEPTEMBER 5, 1982

With Labor Day the next day, the decision was made that we would close the pool for the winter today. It was again unseasonably warm, a high of 84. The forecast for tomorrow was going to be a high in the mid-60s and rain. Closing the pool was a Midwestern yearly ritual every Labor Day weekend. This year, the pool was full of leaves and berries. Leaves and berries from the mulberry tree. The mulberry tree he had killed.

When we moved into the house in 1976, almost immediately, my father began warring with the neighbors behind us. It was brutal.

He would yell over the fence at the woman, the mother of the kids who were close in age to me. "You fucking, ugly bitch."

"You keep your retarded, goddamned kids off of the fence."

"Those tards will fall into my yard. No fucking way."

It was 1982 now, so this had been going on for six years. I felt bad for the neighbors. My father's unabashed contempt toward this woman and her family showed me that he had a complete disdain and lack of any respect for others—a fact I was already well aware of.

The whole war, I believe, had started over a mulberry tree.

The neighbors had had enough. In about 1978, they put up a six-foot privacy fence. Between their fence and our fence was the mulberry tree. According to survey records, the tree was on their property. I feel that they felt threatened enough that they did a rush job on the fence to shelter them from the wrath of Evil Dan, and they didn't have enough time to take the tree down.

Whatever the actual reason, the mulberry tree was still there, lodged between our two fences. He was at war with that tree. I know that sounds psychotic, but consider the source.

At first, he took a chainsaw and attempted to cut the tree right down the middle. That didn't work. The tree survived... and grew. Unbelievable.

He tried several poisons on the tree to no avail. It just kept growing.

As that tree continued to grow despite his abuse, so did his disdain. He was on a mission to kill that tree.

He would rake up the leaves from that tree and throw them over the fence, into the neighbors' yard. He would collect the mulberries that fell off the tree, bring them up into the tree house in our yard, and throw them over the fence. Directly at the neighbor. She was outside and getting pummeled with airborne mulberries. From her own tree. She would scream at him, rightfully so. I would hear words from his mouth that I had never heard before. It was painful to watch and hear. I would have to go into the house. I couldn't take it.

He was becoming more and more unhinged right before my eyes.

The death warrant on the tree's life was signed in the summer of 1980. My father came home from the hardware store with a small, brown paper bag. It was full of copper nails. He also had another container, an old plastic margarine container.

FLASHBACK

SATURDAY, AUGUST 16, 1980

*He is so pissed at that tree. He came home today with a bag of copper nails. I saw him bring the small, brown paper bag down to the workshop. (**There was no lair in 1980. No door. No deadbolt. Just his workshop.**)*

He was sitting at the counter on his stool at the gray, fluorescent magnifying lamp. I was able to just walk into the workshop back then. No trespass required. He sat with his bag of nails. He was putting them into a small, round, plastic container with liquid.

*Of course, I asked, "What are you doing?" (**It was still safe to ask questions in 1980.**)*

"I'm getting ready to kill that fucking mulberry tree. Nothing I've done to it is working."

"What's that?" I inquired.

*"These are copper nails. I'm soaking them in a mild solution of..." (**I don't recall what the solution was. I was nine years old at this time.**)*

"I'm letting them soak for a few days, then watch what happens," he replied.

MONDAY, AUGUST 18, 1980

Dan is off for a few weeks. We're leaving for Hawaii on vacation with my grandma and Sherrie on Wednesday. They get in tomorrow.

He was up a little early. He wanted me to come out back with him.

At our back fence, he had set a small bucket. In the bucket, there was a drill with a drill bit already installed. A clear plastic bag with the copper nails in it. I could see that they had started to oxidize. They had started to turn a greenish color. Also in the bucket was a small, round, margarine container, a hammer, a couple of zip-type plastic bags, and some rubber gloves. The kind my mom used when she did hair color. He had also dragged a few extension cords out to the fence that were plugged into the outlet near the laundry room window.

He proceeded to drill dozens of holes in the base of the mulberry tree. Right through the openings in our chain link fence.

Of course, I was watching intently. I had no idea what kind of magic trick he was going to do. He took out the bag of semi-oxidized nails, an extra clear, zip-type bag, and the margarine container.

He put on not one, but two pairs of gloves. He wanted me to stand back, so I moved back.

He proceeded to take the copper nails out a few at a time. They were still damp from the solution. He dumped a whitish-yellow powder into the zip-type bag. He would take between five and seven nails at a time and drop them into the whitish-yellow powder. He held the bag away from his face when he did this. As soon as he dropped the nails into the bag, I kid you not, there was a bit of smoke. From my memory, I can see the greenish-copper nails turn slightly to a shade of blue.

That is what I remember. A bluish shade.

He would carefully take the nails out of the bag with the whitish-yellow powder and place them into the pre-drilled holes in the base of the mulberry tree, then tap them with the hammer into place.

He did this multiple times. Each time, adding more powder to the zip-type bag. It was some sort of toxic Shake 'N Bake.

When he was done, he dumped all of the remaining powder into the pool.

He looked me straight in the eyes and said, "That is how you kill a mulberry tree. That tree will start dying by the time we get back from Hawaii."

I looked at him wide-eyed. My nine-year-old mind was trying to figure out what I just saw. So, I just asked.

"Okay. I understand the copper nails can kill the tree, but what was the powder?"

Again, he looked me right in the eyes and said, "Cyanide. Potassium cyanide."

I remembered the word "cyanide" from the People's Temple murders and Jim Jones. He had talked about it nonstop a few years ago.

"That is poison, right? Where did you get it?"

"Generous Motors," he replied.

Generous Motors was his slang term for General Motors, the parent company of Electro-Motive Division, where he worked full time. He was always bringing home surprises from Generous Motors: yellow Shell oil drums, mercury, chemicals, and all varieties of little electronic doohickies. Oh yes, and I can add cyanide to the list as well.

He started walking back in the house, through the poolroom, into the basement. He was heading to the workshop. I followed. Things were still somewhat civil at this time.

Once my father had you engaged in a conversation, there was no stopping him. I had asked a question; therefore, I was now engaged. This would take the rest of the afternoon.

So, this conversation continued in the workshop.

MONDAY, AUGUST 18, 1980 – LATER IN THE AFTERNOON

Pretty much the rest of the day was spent with him in his workshop. He bounced around a lot with his stories. He would talk about something that happened on the fire department and then jump back into a Generous Motors story. Then back to his childhood, then jump into a story about hiking. It could be very difficult to follow his stories. You had to listen with a keen ear.

However, once he had ping-ponged around for a while, he focused on telling me a story. One that gets deep and dark, but one I will share it with you now.

DAN'S MILITARY STORY

This story is told in the voice of my father:

So, I joined the army in '69. I joined. I wasn't drafted. I enlisted. I wanted to go to war. Vietnam. I wanted to get the fuck out of Chicago. I enlisted and I was sent off to Fort Lost in the Woods (Fort Leonard Wood). I did my BCT (boot camp training) there.

(I requested my father's military records from the National Archives. I can confirm that he left for Fort Leonard Wood, MO, on June 30, 1969. He did his BCT at Fort Leonard Wood.)

I made it through that basic training. You know how fucking hot it is there in the summertime? Hot, humid, mosquitoes as big as a cat. But I did it. Just as I was about to leave to go to Fort Benning, a couple of bigwigs approached me. And I mean bigwigs. They came up to me and said, "Do we have a job for you!"

They took me into a conference room and had a little talk with me. After our conversation, we all thought it was best if I headed to Oakland. For some, uh, "higher" training.

(My father's military records state that he was supposed to leave for Fort Benning, GA, on September 6, 1969. However, that line on his record of assignments was redacted. There is no official listing of where he was from September 6, 1969, to October 4, 1969.)

So, they sent me out to Oakland. California. The land of fruits and nuts. And let me tell you. I was there for a month or so learning some top-secret shit. They taught me codes and ciphers. I was a good cipher guy. I became a top-notch rifleman. They taught me not only how to disarm bombs, but how to plant them as well. They trained me to be an assassin. You know I can take someone down, permanently, if you know what I mean, with an ordinary pen. I'll teach you that someday.

I learned a lot about chemistry and poisons in Oakland. They taught me how to make my own suicide pill. The suicide pill is just a cyanide pill. You pop it in your mouth and bite down, and it's lights out. I wanted to tell you all of this because we were working with cyanide today. It's a deadly chemical. Just touching it can kill you. It's not a toy.

(Cyanide is kryptonite to people.*)*

Did you catch how I dumped the leftover cyanide in the pool? The chlorine in the pool will neutralize that little bit of it. It's all chemistry, you know.

Do you still remember what I was teaching you about ciphers last year? You still remember what I taught you, right? Just like walking through the woods. Look from the left to the right. From the right to the left. Look backward. Look forward. Always remember to use a mirror too. You'd be surprised at what you can see in reverse in the mirror when you're breaking a cipher.

You still have your name cipher I made you, right? Always keep that. It's important.

Here's something you might not know: the official military line was that there were no nukes in Vietnam. Bullshit. We had them up and ready to go at a moment's notice. I had the nuclear codes. That put a target on my back.

So, anyway, I got a high-up, top security clearance and headed to Fort McClellan.

(My father's military records state that he left for Fort McClellan on October 4, 1969.)

I was at McClellan for a while, then off to Maryland.

(This is all corroborated by his military records.)

You know, when I left for BCT, me and your ma, we broke up. Nothing major. As soon as I left Maryland, I made a stop back here to Chicago. I wanted to marry your mom. I found her. She'd been dating some dick named Bill. They were already engaged. I told her, "You're mine. We're getting married."

I found that dick, Bill, and I beat the shit out of him. (Laughing). We even kept the ring he gave your ma. We ran off to Kentucky and couldn't get married there. So, we got our marriage license here and got married in Berwyn.

(My father's military records corroborate that he left Fort McClellan, AL, on October 31, 1969, en route to Indian Head, MD. He left Indian Head, MD, after his final EOD (Explosive Ordnance Disposal) training on February 7, 1970. My parents got married on February 21, 1970.)

After we got married, we headed off to Okinawa. We were young. I left with your ma, the nuclear codes, and a suicide pill in my pocket. Ya know, if I got caught by the Viet Cong, I was supposed to give 'em my name, rank, and serial number. Bite down on that suicide pill, and it would all be over in about a minute.

My head spun from the weight of his words. This was a lot to take in at nine years old. He spoke with fire in his eyes, recounting every detail of his time in Oakland. I never interrupted. I stayed silent, locked on his every movement, fixed on the rhythm of his voice. The room belonged to him. Every fragment of the story clung to me.

When his tale ended, he showed me his EOD certificate, framed like a relic, dangling from the rafters of the workshop.

I stayed with him in silence, the seconds stretching thin, the air pressing heavy. After a few moments, the quiet grew unbearable. I stood to leave. He stopped me with one last remark.

Hey, Joe, you know this whole conversation we had today about my military training and poison? No, you don't. It never happened. There was no conversation. Understood?

BACK TO SUNDAY, SEPTEMBER 5, 1982

Honestly, I felt bad for the tree. He pounded so many copper nails into that poor, now lopsided and tortured mulberry tree. You could see the base of that tree shining in the sun, ablaze with the copper nails. Bedazzled like clothes that kids wore in that era.

It had taken a few years, but now, in 1982, that tree stood on its last leg. The tree had lost all of its leaves. All of its berries, most of which were now in our pool. And I had to clean them out.

I don't know why, but that poor tree was representative of something else to me. Maybe it was representative of the terror that he unleashed in our lives. Or of the terror he would unleash on the lives of others. A death unleashed by poison. I picture that sickly tree trying to survive but finally dying from the cyanide he had pounded into it.

MONDAY, SEPTEMBER 6, 1982 – LABOR DAY

Anyone from the Midwest, especially Chicago, knows that Labor Day never shows up dressed in sunshine. It arrives soaked, sullen, and chilly, like a seasonal inside joke that never gets old.

Somewhere along the way, someone must have sold their soul to the devil, and this was the rain-soaked payback. And whoever cut that deal must have thrown in Memorial Day as a bonus, because we got the same dreary weather then too.

Not much to report this Labor Day. Dan was relatively quiet today. We cooked out, sort of. Dodging in and out of the rain. The real excitement came later when I spent the afternoon organizing all my brand-new school supplies. There was something sacred about it: the crispness of untouched notebooks, the intoxicating scent of fresh markers and Elmer's glue. I wanted everything just right. Tomorrow was a new beginning. Everything had to be perfect.

TUESDAY, SEPTEMBER 7, 1982 – FIRST FULL DAY

This year was a really big deal. For the first time ever in Robinson School history, things were changing. Sixth grade wasn't just sixth grade anymore. It was something bigger. Something… more serious. We were being taught how to be like high schoolers. Other places might call it junior high, but not Robinson. Robinson had always been a K–8 school. That meant we were still with the same people: same students, same teachers, same classrooms. But something about this year was different.

We were given a homeroom. My homeroom was with Mrs. Judy Jarvis. I already knew who she was because I had seen her in the library last year yelling at some kids. She had a big frizzy perm and was the kind of teacher who didn't play around. She said something like, "Keep your cotton-pickin' hands off…" and I kind of laughed to myself because it sounded funny. But she didn't think so.

She turned right around, stared me down, and said, "What are you laughin' at? You wanna be next?"

I instantly knew she wasn't the type you wanted to mess with.

And just like that, she was my homeroom teacher. She started breaking everything down for us, explaining how things would go from now on. Homeroom with her. Math with Ms. Bernard.

Science with Mr. Zakovec. Social Studies with Mrs. Jones.

Then came the big announcement. For the first few weeks, we would be learning songs. Two Cat Stevens songs: "Moonshadow" and "Morning Has Broken." One kid let out a big, dumb grunt when she said that. Secretly, I was kind of excited. Mrs. Jarvis also said that next Tuesday would be Parents' Day, and a few parents would be coming in to talk about their jobs.

While she was explaining all of this to the class, she kind of gave me this look. A little nod, a wink, and the tiniest smile. I think she might have liked me. It seemed like maybe I had a soft spot in her heart after all.

SATURDAY, SEPTEMBER 11, 1982

I was about to find out why Mrs. Jarvis always gave me that look. That soft, almost protective kind of look. It turns out, she was coming to the house to get a perm. Today, as in this morning. Right here and now. My mom, although fully matriculated into nursing school, still did hair on occasion.

She had agreed to do it. As a kid, you think teachers live in their classrooms. You don't picture them in your basement laughing with your mother with perm rods in their hair. Sitting in the little salon area located just outside of the lair.

I wonder if Mrs. Jarvis has a clue what lies beyond that door?

That day, I was going to a Cubs game at Wrigley Field with my dad. This was strange in and of itself. My father didn't enjoy, play, watch, or engage in any sport of any kind at any time. Ever. I would have rather stayed with Mrs. Jarvis while she got her perm, to be honest.

Dan was oddly charming that morning, even toward Mrs. Jarvis. I caught the tail end of their conversation.

"So nice to meet you, Mr. Drozd. I look forward to seeing you in class on Tuesday for Parents' Day." Mrs. Jarvis was plying him with velvety words.

"Oh, please, call me Dan," he replied. "It's my pleasure." He was plying her back with velvety words.

Who is this now?

He didn't talk like that.

He didn't engage in sports.

What was happening? I was seeing something that to most people would appear normal, but to my trained eye, I saw something different.

Parents' Day. My stomach turned. He was going to show up.

ON THE ROAD TO WRIGLEY

It was over 89 degrees that day. Again, extremely hot for Illinois in September.

We got into the station wagon with the air conditioning that had broken last month en route to Milwaukee.

"Hotter than fuck," he said.

I gave no response. I was once again not sure who I was dealing with.

We took Harlem Avene to I-55, to Lake Shore Drive, going north. Exited and parked somewhere on Addison Avenue.

We got to Wrigley Stadium and sat baking in the sun, watching the Cubs lose to the Montreal Expos. Their defeat felt predictable, but something about the day was most certainly not predictable.

He got me popcorn, hot dogs, and even an Expos pennant. Red, white, and blue.

On the way back, he changed the route. He said there was too much traffic on Lake Shore Drive. We cut across and took Clark Street, the diagonal stretch that slices through the city. We passed the Lincoln Park Zoo.

I made a comment. I said I had never been to Lincoln Park Zoo.

He nodded slowly. "Maybe we'll do a boys' weekend with Justin in a couple of weeks." There was something in the way he said it that felt rehearsed. As if he were already picturing it. Already planning. I should have kept my mouth shut.

We pulled into a gas station. Not just any gas station, 1647 N. La Salle Street. This is an iconic Chicago gas station built in 1971 (like myself), with a retro, space-age look. It's still there today. I don't know why, but something about that place is carved into my mind. Maybe it's because of how he just stood there. Just at the edge of the station, staring down La Salle Street like he was waiting for a sign. I can picture the sun setting and an orange-red glow around him as he stood there. Staring. At what? That image is burned into me.

He filled the car slowly, methodically. When it was done, he walked around, locked the doors tight, and took my hand. Firm grip. Intentional. We crossed La Salle Street. I felt the heat rising from the pavement.

We stayed on La Salle for about a block. Almost perfectly located on the corner is where we entered the Walgreens on Wells Avenue. He bought us each a Coke. That was it. We were in Walgreens for less than five minutes.

Why didn't he just grab a Coke at the gas station? That thought looped in my head like a warning bell. Something was wrong. I knew how to read him by then. His movements, his pauses, the change in his tone. And right then, I felt the shift. That small, imperceptible crack in the routine.

Afterward, he took my hand again. We crossed the street once more, this time on the other side of La Salle Street. We were walking past Moody Bible Institute. Its presence felt cold, hulking. Silent.

We got back in the car. The Coke can was sweating in my hand, but I wasn't thirsty. I was alert. I was learning. I was watching. The sun continued to set, the orange-red halo of a glow. The red wasn't dissimilar to my Coke can from Walgreens on Wells Avenue.

He started to drive again, winding around the block and then Lake Shore Drive. The same Lake Shore Drive which he had said was too crowded just an hour earlier. But there we were, gliding south on Lake Shore Drive under the early evening orange-red halo glow of the sunset. I watched the skyline blur past, Lake Michigan splashing to my left, and I remember thinking, *He goes wherever he wants, whenever he wants. And he does whatever he wants. No matter what he tells you.*

TUESDAY, SEPTEMBER 14, 1982 – PARENTS' DAY

Today was the day.

After a quick morning rehearsal of our Cat Stevens songs and looking at Mrs. Jarvis's fresh new perm, it was straight to math, then science. No social studies at the end of the day. Everyone knew why. It was Parents' Day.

A certain unknown dread built up inside me. What would he do?

What would he say?

Batter up. The first parent for the day was Mr. Plesha. Ken Plesha was my friend Ginger's dad. He was a retired player for the Chicago White Sox. The room buzzed with excitement. He was a legend in our eyes.

And after Mr. Plesha, it was his turn.

Dan. My father. I was unsure of which version of Dan would walk through that door.

He wore his Lyons Police Department uniform. It was perfectly ironed. Creased down the sleeves, crisp collar, badge polished like a mirror. My mom had made sure of that. Of course she had.

He walked to the front of the classroom like he owned it. I started to sweat. It was another 89-degree day in Lyons, and Robinson School didn't have air conditioning. But the heat wasn't just in the air. It was under my skin.

He spoke eloquently. Almost too eloquently. I had never met this version of him before. The polished one. The hero. He talked about his military service, about how proud he was to have served his country. I watched the other kids watch him. Some of them nodded. Some even smiled.

Then he shifted. He told them about his job at Electro-Motive, explaining how he worked on electroplating locomotive engine parts. He slipped in a bit about having been an EMT and fireman at the Lyons Fire Department. How he had served the community in that role as well. Then circled back to say he was now only working "very limited part time" with the Lyons Police Department.

He had rehearsed this.

He wasn't just talking. He was performing.

I sat at my desk, staring at the floor tiles, willing the clock to move faster. I could feel the eyes of my classmates slide toward me. For a moment, though, I felt almost proud.

Then he looked at me.

His face didn't change, but his eyes told a different story. A flicker. Something only I would catch. It was a look as if saying, "See. I can show up as a different character. One that you don't even know."

A few more speeches by parents, and we were off. The bell rang. Time to go. Not so fast. He was still here.

He wanted to walk home with me. This was the one and only time that *ever* happened.

The walk from Robinson to home was less than a block. As we walked, he didn't speak much. He had a heaviness about him. Almost a sadness. I didn't know what it was. I looked up at him in his uniform, and I thanked him for speaking at school. It seemed like the right thing to do.

He looked down at me, almost with a tear in his eyes, and said, "You're welcome, Joey."

What was going on?

TUESDAY, SEPTEMBER 14, 1982 – AFTER SCHOOL

As we walked closer to the house, he turned to me and asked if I wanted to run to Jewel with him.

"Okay," I replied.

We entered the house. I moved quickly, dropping my books with a practiced motion before heading downstairs. On my way back up the steps, I caught the low hum of my mother's voice. She was talking to him, telling him that she had spoken with Mary Ann earlier in the day.

"Today was Mary Ann and Jimmy's anniversary," she said. "They invited us over next Sunday, the twenty-sixth, for a little get-together."

He stopped mid-step, his body stiffening almost imperceptibly. His expression shifted. It wasn't irritation exactly, more the quiet pause of a man running numbers in his mind, weighing time against something unspoken. It was as though the date had collided with an invisible obligation already etched into his calendar.

He exhaled. The air seemed heavier.

"Fuck. Okay. We can head out there after church," he muttered, the words thick, reluctant, shaped by a mind that had already moved elsewhere.

We jumped in the car and headed straight to the Jewel-Osco store on Harlem Avenue.

He told me he had to pick up a few things for the station before he went in later that night, which was also another oddity that day.

He wasn't the type to *pick up a few things for the station...*

We parked in the lot. No cart. That told me we wouldn't be buying much.

Inside, we walked quickly past the aisles. I followed him to the bakery section. He picked up a box of donuts. I remember that clearly.

Then we crossed the store. All the way to the other side. He didn't say what we were getting there.

We got to the Osco side of the store.

He walked up and down the aisles. What was he looking for?

It was as if he were trying to lose me in the store. "Here we go," he said.

He bent forward, both hands moving with purpose, and gathered more than one box of Extra Strength Tylenol, yet fewer than five. The movement was deliberate, measured, as if each box carried weight beyond its contents.

We made our way toward the front. I carried the donuts. He carried the Tylenol. At the counter, he placed the boxes down with a quiet finality. I set the donuts beside them. I remember the count. More than one, fewer than five.

The cashier began to ring the items. A brief pause hung in the air, a momentary stillness that seemed to stretch. He looked at her, the corners of his mouth pulling into a grin that carried both charm and edge.

"You know… they need a Tylenol after I take them down."

The words were steeped in macho bravado, the language of a man comfortable in his role. He was in uniform. His Superman T-shirt was undoubtedly underneath his uniform.

She returned the grin, untroubled, and slid each item into a brown paper Jewel Food Stores 50th Anniversary bag.

"Have a good night, boys," the cashier said with a smile and a wink.

We drove back to Gage Avenue. I remember that drive clearly. We got out of the car and walked into the house.

The bag stayed in the car. He left a few minutes later.

SATURDAY, SEPTEMBER 18, 1982 — AMERICAN SCIENCE & SURPLUS, ACT TWO

He seemed excited. Almost giddy. I had no idea who or what I was dealing with. But one thing was sure. We were going somewhere.

We got in the station wagon and drove down Ogden Avenue to First Avenue. We turned right. We drove through Brookfield, Maywood, and Elmwood Park. Oh yes. American Science & Surplus. Going here wasn't unlike the training missions through the woods, learning the flora, the fauna, and the poisons that grew wild.

I knew one thing that he made clear in a scary, almost childlike voice. He admonished me, "No matter what. Do. Not. Tell Your Mother. Where We Went." Simple enough. Easy peasy.

We were going full incognito.

We turned off onto Northwest Highway. 5700 Northwest Highway. *Here we are again.*

We walked in. I saw my friends, the pickled frogs, still frozen in memories of their former lives. I noticed this time that if you stood back and looked at them from a distance, each frog was in a slightly different position. Scanning them from left to right, they looked like a grotesque cartoon, dancing in slow motion.

I didn't know why we were here. He was asking a few questions of the staff. We could have been there for five minutes or five hours. I lost track of time. I couldn't stop looking at the frogs with empathy. With sympathy. With 11-year-old wonder.

And then off we went.

On the ride home, going the same route that we came, just in reverse, we had a conversation.

He began explaining some things about life. He told me that nothing was as it seemed. People lied. If politicians' mouths were moving, rest assured, they were lying. History was written by the winners.

As if this conversation wasn't dark enough, it grew darker.

"Do you remember a few years back, when all those people died from drinking poisoned Kool-Aid?" he asked casually, his eyes fixed on the road, like he was asking about the weather.

I nodded. "Yes."

"Well," he said, his voice shifting into something low and almost conspiratorial, "the plan to poison them… it actually started out differently."

I said nothing, but I could feel something cold in my chest.

How does he know this? Why is he saying this?

"The man leading that church was Jim Jones. He wasn't a bad guy. He was brilliant, really. He was misguided, yes, but brilliant."

The name struck a chord. I had heard it before. Everyone had. Dan had an obsession with Jim Jones.

"He tried to bring Heaven down to Earth for his followers," he continued. "He was a prophet in his own mind. But his followers rejected him. They mocked his vision. They tried to escape his orbit."

He glanced over at me, then back to the road.

"You know… his original plan was to use antifreeze in the Kool-Aid. But he changed it. He decided to use cyanide instead."

I swallowed hard. "Why?"

"Because he was a merciful man," my father said. "Antifreeze is slow. It's agonizing. It can take days to die from antifreeze. But cyanide? That's quick. By the time anyone realized that anything was wrong… it was already over."

I stared at him, trying to decipher if there was a trace of emotion. Admiration? Pity? Envy? None of the above, except admiration.

He was admiring what Jim Jones had done.

He let the silence settle for a beat before finishing: "And in the end, he took a bullet. For himself."

A thick, uneasy silence filled the car. It was suffocating. My father wasn't just telling me about history. He was delivering a message, one cloaked in riddles and death. I didn't fully understand it at the time, at least not consciously. But I felt the weight of it, like the air had been drained from the world.

He wasn't just recounting a tragedy.

He was praising the efficiency of the poison.

He was praising Jim Jones's mercifulness and his choice of cyanide for its efficiency. And somehow, I knew... this conversation wasn't really about Jim Jones at all.

An eerie quiet enveloped the car. Somber. What I was hearing shouldn't have made sense. But the way he was phrasing it, it was clear to me. My father was telling me that this man who had killed so many people was, in fact, some type of saint. Some type of brilliant, misunderstood genius.

I sat quietly. No response for the rest of the drive home.

That was the moment something in me broke. Whatever veil of safety childhood had offered me was gone. Shattered like jars of frogs, the smell of formaldehyde, and a conversation no child should have had.

SUNDAY, SEPTEMBER 19, 1982

Up early we went, the morning air still cool against our faces, heading for Sunday school and church.

The Church of Christ in Brookfield was a small, tight-knit congregation. The Church of Christ has been my family's spiritual home for nearly four generations through my grandmother's steady devotion. She was a faithful and good woman, her faith woven into the very fabric of our family's history.

In Sunday school, we were immersed in the Ten Commandments. At the Church of Christ, learning meant more than just reciting. It was memorizing forward and backward, perhaps even standing on your head while singing a hymn for good measure.

This particular Sunday marked about the sixth week in our Sunday school lessons on the Ten Commandments. The commandment of the day was the sixth one: "Thou shalt not kill." Ironic. Sunday school and church were usually fun for me. I genuinely enjoyed it. These were safe places, free from the shadows of home. Dan, in whatever mood or shape he took, rarely caused trouble at church. The ride home was another story entirely.

In the Church of Christ, the greatest earthly moment was the one when you stood and declared your decision to follow Jesus and get baptized. The hymn's words still echo in my mind, *"I have decided to follow Jesus... no turning back, no turning back."*

I cannot recall the sermon from that morning, but I remember the feeling. Safe, sheltered within those church walls, a stark contrast to the undercurrent of danger and unease that waited in my own home. Yes, in the house of the Lord, I felt safe.

I just remember that morning, listed on the board to the left of the pulpit, was my favorite hymn. Yes, I had a favorite hymn. Solo a cappella. Voices only.

"Make a joyful noise unto the Lord."

Our a cappella, congregational singing wasn't exactly a joyful noise, but we got by. There it was on the board.

728B.

728B in our hymnal at the time was, "Sing and be Happy."

If the skies above you are gray,
you are feeling so blue,
If your cares and burdens seem great,
all the whole day thru,
There's a silver lining that shines in the heavenly land,
Look by faith and see it,
my friend, trust in His promises grand.
(Chorus)
Often we are troubled and tired,
sick with sorrow and pain,
There are others living in sin,
blest with earthly gain,
Take new courage,
we cannot tell what tomorrow may bring,
When the dark clouds vanish away,
then your heart truly can sing.
(Chorus)
Oft we fail to see the rainbow,
up in heaven's fair sky,
When it seems the fortunes of earth frown and pass us by,
There are things we know
that are worth more than silver and gold,
If we hope and trust Him each day,
we shall have pleasure untold.
(Chorus)

The Church of Christ doesn't, will not baptize an infant. The decision must be made by the individual with their whole heart. It's the greatest joy of any parent in the church when their child decides to "go under."

The church doesn't sprinkle, doesn't pour water over your head. You go under. Completely under. I don't imagine that there is a Church of Christ around that doesn't have access to a body of water. Our congregation, like most, had a baptismal at the front of the building, located directly behind the pulpit. There were stairs behind doors on either side. You got in on one side, and whoever was baptizing you got in on the other.

A warning sign was posted outside of the building: "Warning: Trespassers will be baptized."

The baptismal is about three and a half feet deep, slightly wider than a bathtub, and about seven feet in length. There was a painting of the River Jordan behind it, and there were curtains that were designed to close and then to reopen when it was time.

Today was my day. At the end of the sermon, the preacher asked if there were any prayer requests and if anyone wanted to repent and be baptized and enter the Kingdom of Heaven.

I looked over at Deacon Dan; that is the name I gave to his church persona.

I gave him some subtle head motions that he had been teaching me in the more nefarious corners of his life. He saw them. Eyes wide. He grabbed my hand.

"Are you ready?" he asked.

"Yes," I replied.

He ran to the front of the church and made the announcement:

"Joey, my firstborn, has decided to be baptized today."

There is no occasion more joyous in the Church of Christ than when someone decides to get baptized.

Before I put on my white robe, he asked me, "Do you want me to baptize you, or would you rather have someone else?"

"No. You," I replied.

I changed into my white robe. The congregation gathered close to the baptismal and began singing:

"All to Jesus, I surrender...
To Canaan's Land I'm on my way
Humble yourself in the sight of the Lord."

The curtains opened.

I was on one side of the baptistry in a white robe.

Deacon Dan was on the other side, dressed in wader boots. We met in the middle of the baptistry.

He began, "Joey, my son. Do you believe with all of your heart that Jesus Christ was the Son of God, that He came to this earth, lived as a man, a human, that He suffered and died a cruel death on the cross to atone for your sins, so that your name may be written in the Lamb's Book of Life?"

"Yes," I replied.

"Then, Joey, what is your good confession?" he asked.

"Jesus is Lord," I replied.

"Joey, with your good confession, I can now baptize you in the name of the Father, and of the Son, and of the Holy Spirit. All of your sins will be forgiven, and you will live under God's grace, and your name will be written in the Lamb's Book of Life."

Then, under the water I went.

LATER THAT AFTERNOON – A TOTAL CONTRAST

The morning had been wrapped in hymns, warm smiles, and the soft echo of "Humble Yourself in the Sight of the Lord" still lingering in my head. By afternoon, the warmth of the sanctuary had been replaced by something else entirely.

Almost magically, after my baptism, a feast appeared in the church basement. Church basement food always consisted of fried chicken, macaroni and cheese, mashed potatoes drowning in gravy, coleslaw, and potato salad. After the congratulatory hugs and the quiet magic of my baptism celebration, we drove home. I changed out of my church clothes.

Dan looked at me and asked, almost casually, "Do you want to go on a hike? Just the two of us?"

My mind whispered, *Not really,* but my mouth betrayed me. "Sure."

He packed a bag. Army green, not a backpack but a crossbody style. Details mattered.

We got in the car. I didn't know where we were headed until we pulled into the lot at Saganashkee Slough in Willow Springs, Illinois, the water ringed by forest, the air damp and still.

Dan parked and waited, watching a young couple about 20 feet from the trailhead. He gave me a slight nod, then fixed his eyes on them. I knew that look. When I was eight, he had taught me how to read, write, and crack codes and cyphers, one of his many specialties. Around the same time, he had shown me basic sign language. Now he used it, pressing his thumb between his index and middle fingers. In sign language, it's the letter T, but my stomach told me what it stood for. "T" was for "target."

We stepped out of the car, careful not to make a sound. He let the couple get about a hundred feet into the trail. More hand signals, ones I didn't know, but didn't need to know. I understood.

We followed. At a distance. Always at a distance. Stalking. Watching every move they made, while they had no idea we were there. Dan's rules played in my head: *"Be aware of everything. In front of you. Next to you. Behind you. Always look up. Stick to the left."*

We reached a spot where a fallen tree lay off to the side. He motioned for me to move. He cleared leaves in silence, making a space. From his bag, he pulled a green wool blanket. "Itchy Brother" was what he called the blanket for reasons he never explained. We crouched behind the fallen tree, almost on hands and knees, positioned atop Itchy Brother. Our sightline was just skimming over the edge of the fallen tree.

Then came camouflage netting. He draped it over our heads. The only sound was my heartbeat pounding in my ears.

Why does he have camouflage netting?

And then, we waited. Perfectly still. For at least 20 minutes.

We heard the couple coming back down the trail. They had no idea we were there. We watched them intently. They walked directly in front of us, still with no idea.

I looked at him. I thought if he had some plans for an attack, he just missed his opportunity. Then, without a sound...

He silently leaped up with the netting on him. The netting slid off my head and clung completely to him. The netting almost covered his whole body at this point.

In one swoop, he was over the fallen tree and on the trail. He was holding the netting up so that he didn't trip on it.

He got about five feet behind them. They didn't hear a sound. I had wished that someone had taught them the lessons on observations that I was learning. Perhaps after this encounter, they did.

He got just a bit closer, and…

He made a sound, one that I cannot explain. It was almost like the sound of a wild boar. He made this wild boar-like sound LOUDLY.

The couple turned around. Screamed. Ran for their lives to the parking lot.

He actually stayed on their tail until he reached the entrance to the trail.

They ran, still screaming. Got in their car. I heard the engine start up from where I was, then I heard the tires screeching as they left the parking lot.

He came back to where I was standing. I was stunned.

He calmly packed up the netting and Itchy Brother, and we went back to the car.

That was it. He didn't rush. He wasn't worried that the couple would be around the corner waiting for us. Or worse, the police.

Nothing. Calm as could be.

I was speechless.

He looked to me and said, "That is how you stalk your prey."

WEDNESDAY, SEPTEMBER 22, 1982

Confusion. Fear.

Dread.

These were just a few of the feelings I was having at this point.

Up until then, I had met Regular Dan, Evil Dan, Hyper Dan, and Deacon Dan. At 11 years old, this was a lot to take in. Shit, it's a lot to take in at any age.

That Sunday afternoon, I couldn't tell you which version of him I got during our hike. What I can tell you is that the air around him carried the same unease, the same watch-your-back energy. Violence was the baseline, and on top of that, we were constantly spinning. Mentally, emotionally. Never steady, never still. As my grandma would have put it, we were "not knowin' if we were comin', goin', or already been there."

I see it clearly now, and if I'm being honest, I saw it clearly then. This chaos wasn't random. It was built. Engineered. Custom-made to keep us off-balance, afraid, and second-guessing ourselves. That was the point, to keep us too dizzy to stand, too confused and scared to fight.

And yet, somewhere in me, a switch had flipped. I had started to fall for it once, but not anymore. My mind was made up. The anger burned through the fog. I was done pretending not to see. I was always the one in the room who would look at him and ask, *Am I the only one here who knows this is wrong? Am I the only one who sees this?*

While everyone else turned their heads, I didn't. Not anymore.

I wasn't fooled by him anymore. I knew there was something not right with him. It has taken me the rest of my life after this point to really and truly understand that none of this was normal. It isn't normal for your father to hold a loaded gun to your head, or to your siblings' heads, or to your mother's head. It isn't normal for your father to hunt and stalk strangers in the woods. It isn't normal for your father to give your mom a concussion. It isn't normal for your father to throw your little brother down the stairs. It wasn't normal. None of it was normal.

I was pissed. I was determined to figure him out more than ever. Figure out what he was up to. That is why I decided to break into the lair again, TODAY.

LAIR TRESPASS, ACT TWO

I got home from school a little after 3:15. Dan was nowhere in sight. Was he at the police department? I couldn't say. All I knew was that the keys were hanging in the window again, right there on the hook beside the glass block window, just like before.

I lingered, watching the house. Waiting. Just like he had taught me to do. No sign of him. No sign of my mom. No sign of the kids.

I knew exactly who to ask: The Warden.

I ran next door to Louise's house. In our neighborhood, nothing escaped her notice. At least nothing that happened outside. She was the kind of woman who always seemed to have one eye on the world outside her window, her quiet vigilance woven into the rhythm of our days.

When I was younger, she would watch me after school until Dan came home. We would sit together, sip Squirt, and watch Dina Shore on TV while scooping generous spoonfuls of Neapolitan ice cream. Louise believed there wasn't a single thing that I couldn't handle. She believed in me. I had given her many endearing nicknames over the years: The Italian Firecracker. The Godmother. And, most true to life, The Warden.

There were such age gaps between the kids and me that I was always the one left in charge of watching them. And when Justin reached that point—the point where I couldn't keep him in check anymore—I would take him by the arm (or leg), kicking and screaming, and haul him over to Louise's house. I mean, literally drag him there. She would take one look, shake her head, and settle him down, like only she could.

Louise was a happy part of the fabric of my childhood, stitched into the afternoons and little rescues that kept the days together.

The Warden reported that Justin had a dentist appointment and that they would all be gone for a few hours. I cannot imagine the terror in Dr. Sippy's eyes when he saw Justin was coming in for a visit.

I knew this would take some time.

"Would you like some ice cream, Joey?" Louise asked.

I thought for a second.

"What kind do you have?" I paused and thought that was a bit rude. Sorry, Warden.

"If you have to ask, you must not want any."

Point taken, Warden.

"No. I'd better not. I have some homework to get started."

I couldn't tell her that I was chomping at the bit to get into the lair, now, could I?

There were exactly 13 steps up to The Warden's front door. I had counted them enough times to know by heart. She owned the green two-flat right next door to our house. From those stairs, you could see nearly the whole street if you wanted to.

I ran down those steps to get back to my mission. As I reached the last one, there she was. Patti Ann. Louise's daughter.

Patti Ann previously lived in the flat on the first floor when we moved onto Gage Avenue. I was four and she was nineteen. Patti Ann had this way of making the ordinary feel like something special. That afternoon, she pulled up for a visit in her metallic red Firebird, "Forget Me Nots" spilling from the speakers like it had been written just for her. In my mind, her car was magic. So perfect that I was convinced the music in her car must have been piped in from some secret, better world. It was never the jarring chaos that came from Dan's radio.

We spent time together the way only people who truly enjoy each other's company can. Browsing store aisles, sipping Tab, laughing over nothing. She would take me shoe shopping with her and let me pick out her shoes. She always trusted my choices. Then off to Baskin-Robbins in Riverside for ice cream. She made me feel seen, important.

The night Justin was born in 1978, I was ushered right over to Patti Ann's. We stayed up all night, drinking Tab and talking until the edges of the world felt softer. I can still remember the warmth of those hours, the easy rhythm of her voice. The way being around her felt like stepping into a pocket of safety and light.

Patti Ann got out of her Firebird. Hair. Perfect.

Makeup. Perfect. Clothes. Perfect.

And of course, shoes. Perfect. (I had picked them out.)

She looked like one of Charlie's Angels that Charlie had sent out to Lyons on some secret mission.

"Hi, Patti Ann!" I yelled to her. I wanted to so badly to stay and hang out with her, but I was on a mission. "I've got to get to my homework. I'll see you later!"

Yes, later. I had work to do. But not homework.

I didn't know for sure how long everyone would be at the dentist's office, but I was going in!

Same drill as before. Memorize where the keys were. EXACTLY. Head down the stairs, put the Schlage key into the lock. Turn it.

POW.

I'm in again. I paused, waiting once again to see if an alarm went off, or there may have been a spring gun locked and loaded and ready for my trespass.

None of the above. I reached left.

BUZZZZZZ.

The overhead fluorescents.

Take a quick look and remember exactly where everything is. I looked to the right.

Once again, I thought, *Is that new?*

The answer was yes. That was new.

To the right, inside the lair, where it had previously been an open space near the furnace and water heater, there was now a wall over it.

Not just a wall. It was plywood like you would see over a boarded-up window or door.

Now, what the fuck is he doing? When did he have time to do this? I was just in here not that long ago. How did I not hear him hammering, drilling, and sawing?

It was clear that somehow and someway, he was sneaking under *my* radar. He knew I was observant, so clearly, whatever he was up to, I was *not supposed to know*.

I observed the wall up closely. In a seam, I could see some small hinges. This was now a door disguised to look like a wall. A lair within a lair.

Underneath the gray magnifying lamp were:

A box of my mom's gloves that she would use to apply color. Opened.

A few feet of cellucotton. My mom used this to wrap around people's heads when they got a perm.

A small foldable lock pick. Three yellow bullet trays.

Some clear plastic wrapping had been pushed over to the side.

Now what?

Something about the mystery of what he was doing was truly terrifying.

I took a photo of the area in my mind so that if anything moved, I could be sure to put it back exactly where it had been.

I carefully dragged the stool, which had been placed near the magnifying lamp.

I brought it over to the alcove that was new to me the last time that I was in here. I climbed on the stool. Careful, careful.

I looked on the shelf where the cups had been the last time.

Papers had been moved. No longer were his papers titled, *The Poor Man's James Bond*, in the location they were previously.

The midget cups. Gone.

I guessed that I had been in here, give or take, five minutes. I knew I had a little time. I wasn't aborting the mission this time.

FOUND — TWO MIDGET CUPS. ONE PINK AND ONE WHITE.

The whitish cup that held the mercury had been moved. It was no longer tucked away on the high shelf behind his now missing copies of *The Poor Man's James Bond* but sitting brazenly on the countertop, as if daring me to notice.

But where in God's name was the pink cup? My pulse hammered, breath catching in shallow bursts. The words to 728B flickered through my mind like a broken reel, a nervous, involuntary chant. *Sing and be happy... Press on to the goal...*

I was trying not to pass out. That is how deep the fear ran. If he walked in and found me there, especially if he thought I had uncovered whatever it was he was hiding, I knew with bone-deep certainty he would find a way to erase me.

Those thoughts pressed hard against my ribs, feeding the adrenaline already surging in my veins. I leaned into it, letting it shove me into high gear. No room for hesitation now. Determined.

Focused.

Scanning. Scanning. Scanning.

The mercury was accounted for, but where the hell was the pink cup with the powder?

My eyes swept to the far end of the counter. An old-fashioned wooden toolbox sat there near the magnifying lamp, the kind with a single handle bisecting the middle, open on either side. My hands itched, my ears strained for any sound from outside.

And then, there it was. The pink cup. Silent. Waiting. Just the two of us now. I paused. Once again, I thought I heard the front door. False alarm. Again.

I was standing only a few feet from the new wall/door.

I thought, *I don't know how much time I have. Can I achieve getting behind that wall/door and looking into the pink cup?*

Fuck it.

I'm doing both.

First order of business: open that pink cup.

The thought of the warning played in my head like a reel.

Do. Not. Ever. Touch. That pink cup. EVER!

Screw you, I thought out loud. A phrase I had learned from his mother, my grannie. I held the pink cup in my right hand.

I opened up the Tupperware seal with my left.

Thoughts of *ABORT! ABORT!* raced in my mind. Not this time.

Not today, Satan.

I looked very closely at what was left in the pink cup. I had eyes on it now. Very clearly, I saw a whitish powder. Finer than sand, but not as powdery as powdered sugar.

The midget cup, which had previously been approximately three-quarters full, was now down to an amount that was just enough to even see it. Probably less than 10% of what had originally been there.

This time, I didn't have to try to guesstimate the amount like before, when I could see it through the outside of the cup. I was looking directly at the kryptonite in the pink cup.

In my 11-year-old mind, it seemed like a good idea to stick my finger into the kryptonite.

Maybe to get a little on the tip of my pointer finger and to give a little taste and see if I could recognize this substance.

FLASHBACK

Not too far in the recent past, Dan took me to a gun shooting range. He had just purchased a shiny new .45. I know this range was in Lyons. I had thought that it was for the police only, but I'm not clear on that fact. However, I did see other officers present whom I knew.

He prepped the .45, put a target on the target runner that was in the shape of a human silhouette. He put on his goggles and earmuffs. He put a pair of both on me as well. We stood in the stall.

He hit the button for the target runner. The silhouette was out maybe 40 feet. He fired. BAM.

He hit the target, just to the right of where the heart would be. Good shot.

Now. My turn. I had shot guns with him previously. Much smaller ones, though. For an 11-year-old, this was a big gun. He helped me hold the gun.

Steady. Steady.

He helped me aim the .45. Steady.

Steady.

He helped me pull the trigger.

BAM.

I shot the silhouette right in the crotch.

"Hey, Danny. Your kid's got a pretty wicked shot," someone exclaimed.

I had shot the gun. I disabled my target. Good job. Now, it was time for me to wait it out until he was done.

There was a seating area behind the shooting area. I can picture the green pleather chairs, or maybe they were burgundy. Not important.

I sat in the waiting area, and there was a table with a Mr. Coffee, yellow SOLO Cozy Coffee cups, a jar of powdered creamer, and a glass sugar bowl.

I decided, "Why not? I just shot a .45 and hit the target in the crotch. I'm pouring myself a cup of coffee."

I poured the coffee, put in a little creamer. I had never even had coffee prior to this, but this was the way I saw adults make their coffee.

Next came the sugar. I took the lid off the glass sugar bowl, dipped the plastic spoon in it...

Before I could put the sugar into the coffee, Dan came tearing around the corner. He had been watching me. I wasn't the only observant one in this family.

"What the fuck do you think you're doing?" he yelled at me, nostrils flaring.

The only thing that I could think of was that maybe I wasn't supposed to drink the coffee. Sorry, Officer... I had no idea this special cop coffee was off limits to average citizens. My sarcastic mind pushed this thought to the front of my mind.

My thought made me giggle.

Dan didn't think any of this was funny.

"Don't you EVER. EVER. Take ANYTHING out of an open container like that. Ever again! Do you understand me?" he berated me.

I was embarrassed.

He continued, "You never know what people are up to. Someone could have put poison in that sugar bowl."[4]

I heard his voice in my head from the flashback. The sound was enough to stop my movement. My pointer finger was frozen an inch from the kryptonite before I withdrew it.

I sealed the Tupperware lid and returned the pink cup to the toolbox with exact precision.

There was one last thing I needed to do before leaving the lair. I had to see what lay behind the wall/door.

I traced my fingers along its surface, searching for a weakness. The seam was narrow, almost imperceptible. I worked my fingertips into it, prying and twisting until the sharp edges bit into my skin, leaving thin cuts.

Shit, I thought. *I can't leave any blood here.*

What to do? What to do?

The cuts were thin, like paper cuts.

I ran out to the laundry room and washed my hands.

---

4. John Minnery's book *How to Kill* lists various techniques for murder, and are detailed in Volume 1, published in 1973. Minnery favors cyanide or strychnine (p. 41) and suggests poisoning food, drinks, saltshakers, or sugar bowls (p. 42).

I came back to thoroughly inspect to be sure there was not a trace of blood. There was no blood.

I slipped on a pair of rubber gloves that he had been lying out on the counter. Then, my hard work had paid off. The wall/door opened with a loud *SQUEEEEEEEEAK.*

Inside was a darker space still. The lair within the lair.

The air was stale, the silence pressing.

Only a narrow sliver of light bled in from the overhead fluorescents beyond.

In that dimness, a lone cane-back chair faced our brick chimney. To its side, close enough to touch, rested a rectangular cardboard box. Too short to serve as a table, it seemed placed with purpose. Its position was careful, its stillness deliberate.

The lair within the lair held the kind of emptiness I have only seen in old films. An interrogation room stripped of mercy, stripped of warmth. No bare bulb swung overhead, but I could feel its imagined glare pressing down.

What is this lair within the lair for?

The scene felt staged, but this scene felt like it was already over. Whatever had been set into motion had already happened, and I had arrived too late to stop it.

Now, with these images resurfacing—both the images I buried and the images that drifted unanchored—I ache for the chance I never took. I should have looked longer. I should have read every word scrawled on that box. My eyes glanced, but my fear pulled them away.

I wish I had been brave enough to see that box and that kryptonite for what they were. To act before the chance was gone. That moment will never return.

Instead, I stood there, frozen. I was 11. I didn't understand what I was seeing. I had only a faint idea that it mattered.

I had no idea what the consequences that my failure to move, to speak, or to act would be. I had no idea that my lack of action would change lives forever.

A CHEMISTRY LESSON FROM KURT SAXON

POTASSIUM CYANIDE

"This is a light yellow powder or crystals.

It is an almost instant killer with little taste.

Just a few grains are fatal. There are 437 grains to an ounce or 16 grains to a gram. The beauty part of it is that when potassium cyanide reaches the stomach it reacts with the stomach's hydrochloric acid to generate prussic, or hydrocyanic, acid. The same thing happens when a fellow is strapped into a chair in the gas chamber. They drop the cyanide pellets into a bucket of sulfuric acid and hydrocyanic acid is formed. Actually, a person is his own gas chamber and they could just take a cyanide pellet around to his cell. The elaborate gas chamber is just another example of waste by our state governments."

The Poor Man's James Bond, Vol.1. p. 50

ETHYLENE GLYCOL

"This is simply antifreeze, such as Prestone, Zerex, etc. Always read the can to make sure the ingredient is ethylene glycol. It is a colorless, syrupy liquid with a sweetish taste. It mixes well with both water and alcohol.

Authorities disagree on the lethal dose.

They put it from a half ounce to four ounces.

This is not important, however, as anyone will drink four ounces in his soft drink without becoming suspicious.

It can also be tasted along with what you've put it in. Just wash your mouth out and you will feel no bad effects.

At a party, a half-gallon at a time can be dumped into the punch bowl so that everybody will get his share. Only don't pour it in directly from the antifreeze can. An observer might wonder about you. Instead, put some food coloring or Kool-Aid in it to make it look like grape juice or something and put it in two-quart fruit juice cans."

The Poor Man's James Bond, Vol.1. p. 48

SECTION THREE

CHAPTER FIVE: A FAILED VERSION OF NORMALCY

Before we fully step into Section Three and the next chapter, Boys' Weekend: September 25–27, 1982, I ask you to pause. There is an academic article I have written that must be read first. It isn't optional. It provides the context, the framework, and the dark clarity that is essential for what comes next. Without it, the weekend cannot be fully understood.

Read this article closely. Carry its weight with you as you continue. Then, refocus your lens. See not only through the eyes of the 11-year-old boy I was, but through the sharpened edge of the knowledge this article delivers, alongside the truths already laid out in earlier chapters.

Boys' Weekend isn't a stand-alone idea. It's a crucible where evidence and forewarning collide. Each moment in that weekend grows heavier, more deliberate, when seen through the filter of what you now know.

This is why I stop you here. The past chapters prepare you. The coming article arms you. Take them both with you into the weekend. Don't set them aside because without them, what lies ahead may seem ordinary. With them, you will see it for what it truly was.

FROM RASPBERRY ELIXIR TO CYANIDE CAPSULES: A FORENSIC, PSYCHOLOGICAL, AND LEGAL CASE STUDY OF DANIEL RAYMOND DROZD

Joseph Cibelli, JD Candidate, PhD Student

ABSTRACT

This article examines developmental, psychological, criminological, and legal factors surrounding the 1982 Chicago Tylenol murders, advancing a unified forensic formulation of Daniel Raymond Drozd. The analysis argues that a near-fatal childhood ingestion of a raspberry-flavored sulfanilamide elixir seeded a grievance that, when cued by the mass-marketing of flavored pediatric acetaminophen, was transformed by a psychopathic core into calculated consumer-product tampering. Legal and regulatory implications are discussed.

INTRODUCTION

The 1982 Chicago Tylenol murders remain a landmark in forensic history and consumer safety. Seven people in the Chicago area died after ingesting cyanide-laced

Extra-Strength Tylenol capsules, prompting a nationwide recall and rapid legislative action. This paper develops a comprehensive, stand-alone forensic psychological and legal analysis of Daniel Raymond Drozd as the perpetrator.

LITERATURE REVIEW

Psychopathy

Psychopathy is characterized by interpersonal, affective, lifestyle, and antisocial facets, commonly operationalized by the Psychopathy Checklist–Revised (PCL-R) (Hare, 2003; Hare & Neumann, 2008). Contemporary triarchic accounts parse psychopathy into disinhibition, boldness, and meanness (Patrick, Fowles, & Krueger, 2009). Neurocognitive work implicates abnormalities within amygdala-prefrontal circuitry that underlie callousness and instrumental aggression (Blair, Mitchell, & Blair, 2005).

Antisocial Personality Disorder (ASPD) and Its Connection to Psychopathy

ASPD in DSM-5-TR describes a pervasive pattern of disregard for and violation of others' rights since age 15, typically preceded by conduct disorder (American Psychiatric Association, 2022). Empirically, ASPD shows strong overlap with the lifestyle/antisocial facets of psychopathy (PCL-R Factor 2), whereas psychopathy additionally encompasses interpersonal-affective deficits (Factor 1) such as shallow affect and lack of empathy/remorse (Hare & Neumann, 2008). Thus, many with ASPD are not psychopathic, but most individuals who meet psychopathy criteria also meet ASPD. In forensic practice, ASPD captures chronic behavioral disinhibition, and psychopathy accounts for the cold, instrumental style.

Narcissistic Personality Disorder (NPD) and Psychopathy

NPD entails pervasive grandiosity, need for admiration, and lack of empathy. Grandiose narcissism overlaps with psychopathy within the antagonism domain (entitlement, exploitativeness, arrogance) and, to a degree, boldness (dominance/fearlessness) (Pincus & Lukowitsky, 2010; Miller, Lynam, Hyatt, & Campbell, 2017; Vize et al., 2020). In offender narratives, narcissistic antagonism can provide justificatory frames that rationalize predation.

Product-Tampering Crimes and Regulatory Evolution

Product tampering often reflects grievance, extortion, or ideological motives, exploiting weak points in retail supply chains. The Tylenol case catalyzed tamper-evident packaging requirements for over-the-counter drugs (21 C.F.R. § 211.132) and federal criminalization via the Anti-Tampering Act (18 U.S.C. § 1365).

METHODOLOGY

This work employs a forensic psychological case analysis integrating archival sources, legal materials, and first-person testimony later re-examined through professional training in law and forensic psychology. The approach entails inherent subjectivity; analytic transparency and triangulation across sources are used to mitigate bias.

CASE STUDY: DANIEL RAYMOND DROZD

Early Development and Conduct

Drozd's childhood in Cicero, Illinois, reportedly featured high-stimulation acts (e.g., detonating M-80s in sewers; hauling a car engine into a living room), truancy, theft, arson, and general irresponsibility. Such behaviors are prototypical of conduct disorder trajectories and load on the PCL-R lifestyle/antisocial facets (Hare, 2003).

The 1982 Cue: Children's Acetaminophen as Symbol

By the early 1980s, child-friendly acetaminophen products (e.g., flavored liquids and chewables) were ubiquitous. The 1982 release of Children's CoTylenol formulations served as the trigger that transformed grievance into calculated mass murder. Publicly, they signified pediatric progress. For Drozd, they re-animated the original betrayal. Sweetened medicine marketed to children. The symbol returned at retail scale, and grievance met opportunity.

PERSONALITY AND MOOD FORMULATION

ASPD as Behavioral Scaffold

Across the lifespan, Drozd's pattern reflects deceitfulness, irresponsibility, property destruction, theft, and disregard for safety, behaviors consistent with ASPD (American Psychiatric Association, 2022). ASPD provides the enduring behavioral scaffold that made a tampering campaign pragmatically feasible.

Psychopathic Core: Organized, Callous Predation

The offense required foresight, patience, and emotional detachment: acquiring capsules, contaminating, resealing, and redistributing bottles across stores, and accepting indiscriminate victims. These features align with psychopathy's interpersonal-affective coldness joined to instrumental aggression (Hare, 2003; Hare & Neumann, 2008; Patrick et al., 2009; Blair et al., 2005).

Narcissistic Antagonism and Grandiosity

Descriptions of grandiosity and entitlement are consistent with NPD features. In the case formulation, narcissistic antagonism contributed to moral disengagement, an 'avenger' identity rationalizing collateral victims (Pincus & Lukowitsky, 2010; Miller et al., 2017; Vize et al., 2020).

PSYCHOPATHY VERSUS SOCIOPATHY

While sociopathy emphasizes environmentally emergent, volatile aggression, psychopathy entails affective coldness and organized predation. Drozd appears to embody a developmental arc from chaotic sociopathic volatility in youth to psychopathic instrumentalism in adulthood.

SENSORIMOTOR NEUROPATHY AND PERSONALITY TRAJECTORY

Sensorimotor neuropathy itself does not produce psychopathy. Yet early toxic injury can interact with psychosocial adversity to blunt affect and shape personality development. In this case, the toxic-trauma dyad, elixir poisoning amid an unstable environment, may have facilitated emotional detachment while grievance supplied aim (Schep et al., 2009; O'Brien et al., 2014; LoPachin & Gavin, 2015).

LEGAL AND REGULATORY ANALYSIS

At the time of the murders, consumer packaging emphasized child-resistant closures. The crimes exposed vulnerabilities in retail supply chains and catalyzed federal tamper-evident packaging requirements for over-the-counter drugs (21 C.F.R. § 211.132) and the Federal Anti-Tampering Act (18 U.S.C. § 1365). The sequence illustrates catastrophe-driven lawmaking: tragedy → rulemaking → statute.

CRIMINOLOGICAL THEORIES APPLIED

Strain Theory (Merton, 1938): Early poisoning forged enduring grievance against pediatric pharmaceuticals.

Differential Association (Sutherland, 1947): A milieu normalizing deviance reinforced antisocial learning.

Routine Activities (Cohen & Felson, 1979): Retail supply chains offered suitable targets lacking capable guardianship (pre-1983).

Neutralization (Sykes & Matza, 1957): Victims framed as collateral. A denial of the victim and an appeal to higher loyalties.

DISCUSSION

The raspberry-flavored elixir served as the foundational symbol. Sweet medicine as poison, later mirrored by child-friendly acetaminophen at scale. Personal grievance intersected with supply-chain vulnerabilities, prompting durable regulatory change.

LIMITATIONS AND ETHICAL NOTE

This analysis is a forensic formulation. Sensitivity to victims and their families is paramount; the purpose here is explanatory and preventive, not sensational.

CONCLUSION

Psychopathy converted a childhood symbol of betrayal into an adult strategy. Law and regulation responded by transforming packaging and creating a federal anti-tampering regime. The case remains a seminal junction of psychology, criminology, law, and consumer safety.

SEPTEMBER 25-27, 1982 – BOYS' WEEKEND
THE MORNING OF SATURDAY, SEPTEMBER 25

Dan was up early. He allowed everyone else to sleep in. I heard him humming in the kitchen as he made French toast. The smell moved through the house, a combination of frying grease with a faint sweetness.

I remained in bed for a few extra minutes, noting the calmness of the morning.

I heard my mom and Liz in the kitchen. A few minutes later, Justin entered as well.

Dan called down the stairs, "Joe, French toast is done. Come and get it."

I stayed in bed several more minutes before getting up. I turned the corner and walked slowly up the stairs, stepping over the creaky stair halfway up. I turned right and entered the kitchen. The sun was shining.

Dan had plated the French toast. On the island in the kitchen were milk, orange juice, coffee, and a bottle of Mrs. Butterworth's syrup. Dan was mixing milk and powdered sugar in a small container. I watched him closely, noting each movement.

I wondered if what he was mixing was actually powdered sugar or the leftover kryptonite. We ate in the dining room. We rarely ate there.

We had French toast with syrup and the powdered sugar mixture. After breakfast, I showered to remove the greasy smell.

The plan for the day was to visit the Lincoln Park Zoo. My mom and Liz stayed home.

I wore jeans, a burgundy polo shirt, rust-colored suede Great American Shoe Store lace-ups, and brought a hoodie. Justin wore jeans, a navy turtleneck, and a navy hoodie. Dan wore jeans, boot- style shoes, his Superman T-shirt, and his red Lyons Fire Department jacket.

We left in the Buick station wagon at approximately 10:15 a.m. Dan drove down Harlem Avenue to Interstate 55 north, then to Lake Shore Drive north, and then to LaSalle Street.

We passed the iconic gas station that is etched into my soul.

We wound around for a bit. I think he was looking for street parking. No such luck. We drove up to Fullerton and turned onto North Cannon Drive. This is the main lot at the zoo. We parked and entered at the East gate.

LINCOLN PARK ZOO

As we entered the zoo, I noticed couples holding hands. Dads carrying kids on their shoulders. People laughing and having fun.

All I could think was that this day seemed off for us. The lack of normalcy in our lives was screaming for attention. This wasn't normal. This pastel, water-colored version of my family didn't exist. It felt staged, constructed in a way that only drew more attention to how foreign it was.

We toured around the zoo for probably 40 minutes. My biggest moments that day were in the primate house, the waterfowl lagoon, and the farm. We meandered through paths, the air thick with that autumn blend of crisp coolness and faint decay.

We eventually ended up at the Farm-in-the-Zoo. This is where our version of normalcy kicked in. Predictable in its unpredictability.

At the farm area, there was a man selling Lincoln Park Zoo balloons. Justin wanted one. He was beginning to get cranky.

With a touch too much performance in his voice, Dan reached into his pocket for his wallet. He pulled it out, glanced inside, and said, "Oh, shit. I didn't bring any cash today. I must have left it at home."

Something in me immediately sharpened. The words landed wrong. The tone was wrong. He was acting, and not well. My mind locked onto the question. What was he up to?

He said, "Okay, guys. There is a Dominick's down the street. I'm going to run down there and cash a check." His instructions followed quickly. "Joey, you stay with your brother. I'll be right back." Then, as if to smooth it over, "We'll get some balloons and then eat some lunch when I get back."

This abnormality was almost more familiar than the false normalcy of the morning. It was the off-kilter rhythm I knew too well.

I watched him. My eyes didn't leave him as he exited the farm gate and turned left onto Stockton Drive. From the bench where I sat with Justin, I could see his back as he walked away. His red Lyons Fire Department jacket stood out like a flare in the crowd, but with each step, it became smaller and smaller.

Ten minutes.

Twenty.

Thirty.

Forty minutes.

I sat at the farm with Justin. Alone. He was crying. He was cranky. I didn't know where our father had gone.

Stay calm, I told myself. The words sounded steady in my head, but my chest was tightening. Each minute was an accusation. Forty minutes of unanswered questions and holding onto a composure that was starting to slip.

I was 11 years old. I was stuck in a place I had never been before, with a child not even four years old. My mind started to turn in directions I didn't want it to go. *How do we get home from here? How do I explain this to a stranger if I have to?* I could feel my pulse in my ears.

We were in the city. Alone. Scared. The crowd moved around us, the noise of the farmyard animals clashing with the sound of children's voices and laughter. It all felt distant, like I was inside a bubble no one else could see.

I didn't have a watch. The times I have listed above are estimates. Generous ones. I sat with Justin for what I believe was at least 45 minutes. Every one of those minutes was another reminder that we had been left there.

Where did he go?

Then I saw it. That red jacket, moving toward us on Stockton Drive. From the bench where I sat, I watched him come closer. The sight should have brought relief, but instead, I felt my stomach twist.

He came around the corner, smiling, and said, "Good job, Joe."

Fuck off, I thought.

Even now, as I write these words, my anger builds. These images haven't dulled. They have only grown sharper, more defined. This wasn't just a moment of being left alone in an unfamiliar place. It was another crack in the already shaky ground beneath me. I have never forgotten exactly how it felt to sit there, waiting for his return. Wondering exactly what he was up to.

And just like that, he was back. Emerging from wherever he had gone, as if absence could be erased by mere reappearance. The world, or at least the fractured version we inhabited, was expected to resume its prescribed order.

He offered no explanation, no apology, merely the perfunctory gesture of acquiring a few Lincoln Park Zoo balloons. Bright, helium-filled distractions paid for in cash.

We walked in silence back to the car, the day's brief novelty already curdled into something bitter. Lunch was a graceless affair. Pimento loaf on thick slices of Butternut white bread, the cloying saltiness of Jay's potato chips, and the burn of warm Coca-Cola on the tongue. The food sat between us like an uninvited guest, each bite weighted with the knowledge that I had been abandoned. Left in the dubious company of Justin for precisely 45 minutes. I was pissed. That was it.

I watched him with a forensic precision that only resentment can sharpen. The set of his jaw, the almost careless movements as he unpacked the lunch, the way his eyes never quite met mine. In those moments, my irritation wasn't a flare. It was a slow, corrosive seep. I was too young to name it, but old enough to recognize its texture.

Where the fuck did he go?

Poisons offer a quiet alternative to things that go *boom* in the night…

The clock read 1:30 when I finally spoke, my voice a study in practiced neutrality. We headed back to Lyons along the same route we had taken into the city, the landscape reversing itself in the windshield. A cinematic rewind of streets and structures. There it was.

The road home didn't feel the same. It never did after a day like this. Every mile carried the residue of my anger, each turn a reminder that time, once squandered, cannot be restored. We drove in reverse, but nothing in me was returning to where it had been. Again, I was pissed.

BACK ON GAGE

We arrived back on Gage sometime between 2:15 and 2:20, the neighborhood caught in that peculiar lull between afternoon brightness and the first hint of evening light. My anger, though not entirely extinguished, had retreated to a slow simmer. Less a blaze than an ember, buried deep but still capable of reigniting at the smallest provocation.

Next on the day's unspoken itinerary: the movies. It appeared that Hyper Dan had returned, in full, volatile force. The abrupt transitions between his incarnations, merciless one moment, effusive and restless the next, were nothing short of exhausting. It was like living with a man whose moods were marionettes, jerked about by unseen strings and an unseen puppeteer.

On his way to the lair, he stopped at my bedroom door. He leaned in, the casualness almost studied.

"Hey. Thanks for staying with your brother. I'm proud of you for how you step up. I really am." His words floated there, deceptively gentle, as if a simple acknowledgment could undo the sting.

"You wanna go to the movies tonight?" he added quickly, that familiar undertone of urgency in his voice. The plea of Hyper Dan, who never wanted to be alone. Who filled every silence with motion, every stillness with noise.

Before I could respond, he sweetened the invitation. "You know the re-release of *Star Wars* is playing at Yorktown?"

Of course, I knew. This was the 1982 re-release of *Star Wars: Episode IV – A New Hope*. For those who don't keep track, it was the original *Star Wars*, the one that had altered the cinematic landscape, now wearing the label *Episode IV* like a royal title. I was more than familiar with its legacy. My father had taken me to see it over 30 times since its 1977 debut. This was before we owned a VCR, before films could be summoned at will. Each screening was an event, a deliberate journey. This re-release had been running for a month or two, mostly on weekends, a familiar beacon.

For us, *Star Wars* was our demilitarized zone, a kind of neutral ground where the weapons of our conflicts were left at the door. Once inside the darkened theater, we became uneasy allies. We shared popcorn, sipped Cokes, and unwrapped candy, the sound of crinkling paper and fizzing soda mingling with John Williams's swelling score. We sat side by side in the enveloping dark, our eyes forward, our words minimal, as if conversation might shatter the fragile armistice the film provided.

And so, in that moment, I decided to lay down my arms. The thoughts of being abandoned at the zoo were still there, sharp-edged and vivid. But I was willing, however tentatively, to call a truce.

Hyper Dan thundered up the stairs. His feet struck the wood in rapid succession, each impact sharper than the last until he hit the one treacherous step, the creaky one, halfway up. That step always announced a person's presence, no matter how light their tread. But there was nothing light about him in this moment. He burst into the kitchen with the force of an incoming tide, his voice already mid-declaration, as if the words had been waiting impatiently to be unleashed.

"My son and I are going to the movies!" he proclaimed, the sentence carrying both the exuberance of an announcement and the authority of a decree. I mentioned earlier that he had been treating me like a Don. It was like I was his best/only friend right now.

My mother and Liz were in the living room, caught in that quiet, end-of-day stillness. Justin was napping, his small, rhythmic breaths a counterpoint to the sudden eruption of energy upstairs.

The house had its own pulse, and Dan had just sped it up.

VILLA NOVA

By 4:30, the momentum had shifted again. Hyper Dan had planted himself by the phone, punching the dial with impatient precision, dialing Villa Nova Pizza in Stickney. His voice boomed into the receiver, a mixture of command and habit.

"I need an extra large," he said, drawing out the words as though their size alone demanded respect. "Half cheese and half sausage." Here, the word sausage was rendered in the proper Chicago vernacular, "sah-sage." "I want 'em well done. Give 'em an extra turn in the oven."

He wanted them to know he meant it. No limp crust, no pale cheese. Pizza should be crisp at the edges, molten at the center, and substantial enough to burn your fingertips if you were careless.

He seemed almost buoyant after the call, pacing the house with that restless energy that made the air around him feel charged. About half an hour later, he was gone. Or at least I think he was. I heard the door, the shift in the floorboards, the faint rumble of the car as it backed down the driveway. Whether I actually saw him leave or simply pieced it together from the sounds, I couldn't say. But in my mind's eye, he was already halfway to Stickney, chasing the scent of blistered cheese and browned crust, the anticipation of pizza just one more piece in the peculiar prelude to our night at the movies.

STAR WARS

I cannot recall the precise moment of our departure. The day's light had begun its slow retreat, surrendering to the weight of dusk.

Dan still wore his Superman T-shirt, the colors bold against the crimson Lyons Fire Department jacket.

I remained in my burgundy polo shirt, the fabric holding the faint scent of the afternoon. We made our way toward Yorktown Mall.

It had become a ritual, an unspoken agreement etched into the fabric of our outings. Whether the destination was Yorktown or North Riverside Mall, there would be a pause before the theater.

Dan would pull the car to the side and step into a store. A Jewel. An Osco. A Woolworth. A Walgreens.

He would emerge moments later with candy for us to smuggle into the darkened cinema. This tradition was his creation, and he guarded it with care.

The Yorktown theater stood apart from the mall itself, a structure separated by an expanse of asphalt.

That night, the powder blue Vega carried us across the lot before he eased it into a space. The engine remained running.

"It's getting really chilly out. I want to leave the car running," he told me.

His voice carried the softness of reason, yet I recognized the command beneath it. I stayed in my seat. The air carried a bite that hinted at winter's distant approach.

Temperatures had rested in the 50s that day, the kind of cool that seeps into your bones without warning, but not yet cold enough to leave the car running.

I complied. There was no alternative.

He vanished into the evening's dimness. Ten minutes passed, though they felt longer.

He returned with both hands heavy, his jacket pockets swollen with contraband. Boxes of Hot Tamales and Jujubes for me, Dots and Good & Fruity for himself.

We crossed the parking lot together, the theater lights spilling across the blacktop like a muted halo.

He parked once more, this time closer to the doors.

We purchased our tickets and secured our popcorn. He drenched his in butter. I abstained. The slick and greasy taste had always turned my stomach.

We found our seats. The opening crawl of *Star Wars* lit the room in gold.

We ate. We sipped our Cokes. We consumed the sweetness and salt as the galaxy unfolded before us.

The night appeared unremarkable, yet time sharpens truth.

I'm now certain that his brief absence on the other end of the parking lot had a purpose beyond candy.

He had planted a bomb at the mall.

Poisons offer a quiet alternative to things that go *boom* in the night…

SUNDAY, SEPTEMBER 26, 1982

The day started with Sunday school and church.

There were more congratulations on my baptism from friends not in attendance last week.

Sunday school marked week seven in the study of the Ten Commandments. The verse was simple, etched in stone for millennia: "Thou shalt not commit adultery." The words sat in the air, immutable and absolute, yet already diluted by Dan's hypocrisy before the service had even begun.

The morning service offered little in the way of grandeur. No hymns worthy of recall. No moments that stirred the soul. Yet there he stood. Dan. The church treasurer, the deacon, the man whose hands had touched death in ways that no one in the pews could imagine. Today, he was Deacon Dan in full form, stepping to the front to deliver the communion prayer with a voice steady and solemn.

"Let us pray," he began. The tone was deliberate, almost tender.

"Dear Father, as we prepare to partake in this memorial of the last supper, we think of the evening before your betrayal. Partaken in the upper room. You said to your disciples, 'Take and eat, every one of you. This is my body, which has been broken for you.'"

He would break the bread with practiced ease. The gesture appeared reverent, but now I cannot help but see the other set of hands. Those same fingers reaching into boxes, handling capsules, sealing away the unseen ruin within them.

"'Also, take of this cup. This cup represents my blood. The blood of the new and everlasting covenant, which is poured out for you for the forgiveness of sins.'"

He lifted the cup, took a sip. The congregation followed. The act was ritual, but the irony cut deep. The man was drinking in remembrance of a savior while carrying the knowledge of his own unconfessed crimes.

"'Truthfully, I say to you. Unless you eat of this flesh and drink of this blood of the Son of Man, you have no eternal life.'"

He pressed on without faltering. "This is a time of remembrance of your death, burial, and resurrection. Let us each look into our own heart and conscience to determine for ourselves if we are worthy.

"In Jesus' name we pray. Amen."

He moved then to the logistics, passing the trays of bread to the others, usually four men. They ascended the aisles, distributing the broken pieces row by row. The four returned to the front, and the trays of grape juice followed the same route.

From the pews, it was an act of service. From where I sat, it was an act of theater. An unholy performance staged in the house of God led by a man who could bless the bread in the morning and poison a bottle by nightfall.

After church, he settled himself at the back of the church. He sat behind the modest counter where the day's offerings were tallied. The light filtering in through the high windows fell across his hands. His right hand bore a faded tattoo of a cross. A tattoo that he had previously told me started out as *something else.* He never gave an explanation for that.

His hands moved with the precision of habit. He was counting the money. Adding the checks. An act I had seen him perform countless times before.

He worked in a steady rhythm. He would lick the tip of his index finger with a quick, practiced motion, then flip each check forward in the stack. His other hand would guide them beneath the firm stamp, the ink pressing into the paper with a crisp, final sound. Each motion was identical to the last. Efficient. Mechanical. As if his body had learned this task so well, it no longer required thought.

It was this day that my eyes caught something they had never caught before. This wasn't the last time this would happen. I was continually studying him. There was a small wooden mailbox that stood to the right of the counter. A humble thing unnoticed by most. But today, it held something that pulled at my attention.

A letter.

The plain white envelope bore the church's address neatly written across the front. The return address was one I recognized instantly. It belonged to our neighbor. My gaze traveled to the back flap, and there, scrawled in red marker, were words that struck with the force of a whispered accusation shouted in an empty room:

Dan is the Devil

The letters bled slightly into the paper, as though the hand that wrote them had pressed hard enough to tear the envelope.

I reached for it. Slowly. Carefully. My fingertips brushed the edge, but before I could claim it, a shadow fell over my hand. Deacon Dan had seen me. His movements, usually deliberate, now carried the speed of someone cutting off a threat before it could breathe.

He seized the envelope from my grasp. His fingers were firm, almost bruising. He looked me directly in the eyes, the kind of look that wasn't a question but a warning. His pointer finger rose, then moved side to side in a silent command.

"No. No," his fingers stated.

I froze.

Without breaking my gaze, he tore into the envelope. The sound of ripping paper seemed louder than it should have been. Each tear was deliberate, shredding not just the message but the possibility of it ever being read again. He reduced it to jagged pieces, his hands working quickly and decisively.

When the last scrap was gone, he turned and dropped them into the wastepaper basket with the same unremarkable efficiency he had shown while stamping checks minutes earlier. The gesture was final, yet entirely casual. As if erasing words like *Dan is the Devil* was no more than clearing away the remnants of a Sunday bulletin.

Somebody was on to him. Somebody knew something. Somebody was trying to tell somebody something.

Dan is the Devil weren't kind and sentimental words. They were a truth.

"You know tampering with the mail is a federal crime," he admonished me.

AFTER CHURCH

Dan was still seething from my handling of the letter. His irritation sat heavy in the space between us, an invisible weight pressing into the air as we climbed into the Buick. Evil Dan was at the wheel now. Not the smooth, smiling Deacon Dan, but the other one. The one whose patience could evaporate in an instant.

From the passenger seat, my mother reminded him that today was the party at Mary Ann and Jimmy's. Her tone was casual, almost conversational, as though she were speaking to a man who could still be reasoned with.

Justin made a small sound in the back seat. A murmur. A restless exhale. It was nothing, but in that moment, nothing could feel like provocation.

Evil Dan's head snapped around. His gaze swept across all three of us with a precision that felt like a blade. Liz was only a little over one, strapped into her car seat, her tiny face lit with the innocence of a smile.

Then his eyes changed. Whatever humanity had been in them a second earlier drained away, leaving something darker, flatter, more dangerous. His nostrils flared, and without warning, his arm shot back. His hand found Justin's mouth in a slap so sharp it cracked through the air like the splitting of wood. I could almost hear the grind of a tooth under the force.

We froze. The car was silent except for the echo of that blow hanging between us. Then came the explosion.

"Shut the fuck up. All of you. What do I have to do to get some quiet from you fucking assholes?"

His voice was a weapon. Each word was delivered with the precision of someone accustomed to the power of fear.

Justin's eyes welled. Liz's smile collapsed into a wail, her cries high and piercing. I stayed still, silent, my body rigid against the seat. There was nothing to do but wait for the next blow.

Whether it came from his hand or his mouth, nobody could know.

He turned forward again, slamming the key into the ignition. The Buick roared to life, and he peeled out of the parking space with an acceleration that threw us all back against our seats.

"Mother fuck. I can't get a minute of peace around these fuckers. Now we have to go out to fucking Warrenville for the Pollacks' anniversary party."

The car hurtled forward, his anger still coiled and alive in the confined space. No one spoke.

SUNDAY LUNCH

After the mind-numbing fear that had saturated every inch of the car, we made a stop. The Brookfield Restaurant.

Today, it goes by the name Tony's. It sits on the corner of Ogden and Prairie Street, just a few blocks from the church. In its own way, the building has a certain small-town infamy, a kind of lasting presence. A life-sized fake cow stands on the roof, a silent, absurd monument that has seen decades of comings and goings.

We went in. Liz was still crying, her small body trembling in the aftermath of the drive. Justin sat rigid, the flush from the slap still spread across his cheeks, his eyes cast downward. I was locked inside my own head, thoughts running tight circles.

But Evil Dan was hungry, and hunger for him wasn't just a physical state. It was a command that demanded the compliance of everyone around him. The world needed to stop spinning on its axis whenever he wanted something.

I no longer remember what anyone else ordered, only that his selection was the same as always: a turkey club. It was the kind of order so automatic it was muscle memory. When the plates arrived, he did what seemed unthinkable.

He said grace. Not a hurried mutter, but a practiced, polished blessing. His voice was smooth, even warm. The same voice he used when leading the prayer at church, the same voice that could convince strangers they were in the presence of a good man.

"Let us pray."

I could hear my grandmother's words in my mind, as clear as if she were sitting across from me:

Hypocrite.

My mind, however, returned to *Dan is the Devil.*

He thanked the waiter.

He said "please" and "thank you" when asking for more water.

Every surface interaction was perfectly polished, like a silver-plated spoon hiding the rotted brass beneath its shine.

And then he began to eat.

If I had ever doubted my grandmother's judgment, those doubts withered right then. I watched him lift the sandwich, his jaw working as he tore into it. I could hear every bite: the grind of his teeth through the toasted bread, the squish of tomato, the wet smack of his mouth as he chewed. He slurped at his drink between mouthfuls, the sound amplified in my mind until it was all I could hear. Each bite seemed to stretch into an act of domination, as if the food itself was another thing he could control.

With every chomp, every swallow, my disdain for him deepened—if such a thing were even possible. Watching him eat felt like watching the inside of his character. Messy, loud, unrefined, and absolutely without shame.

It was a mind fuck of a lunch. Around us, the restaurant hummed with the normal rhythms of other people's Sundays. But at our table, reality was fractured. One half violence, the other half performance. I was stuck in the middle, trapped in the act of watching a man devour his meal as if nothing in the world had happened at all.

TO WARRENVILLE... AND BEYOND

Evil Dan's mood was the only steady thing that day. Steady in its volatility, anchored in its instability. The tone he had set since after church hadn't shifted an inch.

We returned to Gage for a quick wardrobe change, as if the next act of the Evil Dan show required a new costume. Clothes changed, faces arranged into something passable for public viewing, we prepared for the drive. I hoped, naively, that maybe, just maybe, the mood might lighten.

It didn't.

The ride was rough, the kind of quiet that was loud in all the wrong ways. We arrived at Mary Ann and Jimmy's, the aroma of barbecue greeting us before the front door even opened. Cake sat on the counter beside other tempting dishes, but even those friendly offerings couldn't sweeten the heaviness in the air.

Randy and Mary were already there. They lived just a few minutes away. I took a seat on the couch in Mary Ann and Jimmy's living room. My eyes roamed the space. Not snooping, just looking. Trying to distract myself from the oppressive weight radiating from Evil Dan's presence. The air itself seemed altered by him, denser, heavier. There was laughter now and then, but it was the brittle kind, the kind that cracks too easily because it's built over discomfort.

In their record collection, I noticed Olivia Newton-John's "Physical" single sitting on top. Beneath it, her *Totally Hot – Dancin' Round and Round* album. I made a comment to Mary Ann, "I like your taste in music." She winked at me.

I think she knew. I think she always knew. Mary Ann understood that my father wasn't right. She carried that knowledge quietly, with a kind of protective grace. She had a generosity about her, an empathy that made her different from most adults in my world. She has always been special to me for that reason.

The party went on far too long. I'm certain our hosts were counting the minutes until we left so they could breathe again, so the air in their home could return to normal.

Eventually, I saw Evil Dan in conversation with his brother Randy. They were too focused, too deliberate. Randy turned the moment into a beer run. The nearest grocery store, Frank's Finer Foods in Winfield, was less than two miles away.

Evil Dan and Randy left together. Dan wore his red Lyons Fire Department jacket, the one that could serve as a shield, a disguise, an unspoken badge of trust. Randy had on a leather jacket. They left in the Buick. Gone for nearly two hours.

I'm not suggesting that Randy was part of anything sinister. He was, that day, more of a decoy. Or was he? His presence provided Evil Dan with cover, the kind of alibi built not with words, but with optics. Two brothers were running an errand. Nothing suspicious. Nothing to see here.

And really, who would question a man in a fire department jacket? Who would see danger in that? I mean, really. Who would?

Poisons offer a quiet alternative to things that go *boom* in the night…

MONDAY, SEPTEMBER 27, 1982 – TEACHERS' INSTITUTE DAY. NO SCHOOL

We made it back alive from Warrenville. After Dan and Randy's nearly two-hour excursion, which, by the way, no one asked about.

My brain started saying once again, *This isn't normal. None of this is normal.*

STOP THE PRESSES: THURSDAY, AUGUST 14, 2025. 3:21 P.M.

I need to take a slight detour.

For years, I have been immersed in this investigation. Even before Dan died. I have done numerous interviews with people who knew him or the family, or who worked alongside him. Countless messages sent, calls made, questions asked. I have given my email and phone number to dozens of people, each one a possible key to the locked lair door in this case.

Today, as I was writing about Monday, September 27, 1982, my cell phone lit up. The number displayed was (937) 717-****, Springfield, Ohio.

I answered. "Hello?"

There was a pause. Too long to be accidental. Then a voice, warped and distorted, as if passed through a scrambled signal, broke the silence.

"You're on the right track. Your dad did it." Clear. Unmistakable.

Then silence.

The call lasted exactly 14 seconds.

I hit Redial immediately. Verizon's automated voice answered instead. "Welcome to Verizon Wireless. The number you dialed has been changed, disconnected, or is no longer in service. If you feel you have reached this recording in error, please check the number and try your call again."

I called again. And again. The same recording.

I searched the number online. The trail led to a dead end. The last recorded owner had died in 2020. Whoever called me today was a ghost or, more than likely, using a burner number.

Someone, somewhere, wanted me to know that I was getting close.

MONDAY, SEPTEMBER 27, 1982 – TAKE TWO
7:30 A.M.

Today was a Teachers' Institute Day at Robinson. No school. The absence of a school day gave the morning a strange, unanchored feeling, as if time itself had been loosened from its moorings.

The sun was up at 6:43 a.m. I slept until about 7:30.

Dan was home. Once again, he was making French toast in the kitchen. Same drill as before. The smell crept into the hallway, rich and warm, yet somehow cloying.

He was in a good mood this morning. This man was like an elevator. Up. Down. Up. Down. Repeat.

The swings in him were always abrupt, almost mechanical. When he rose, you never knew how far the drop might be.

Today we had Hyper Dan.

He had been talking about taking Justin and me to Busse Woods as part of our boys' weekend.

According to the Forest Preserve District of Cook County:

"The 3,558-acre Ned Brown Preserve—popularly known as Busse Woods—is one of the largest and most diverse locations in the Forest Preserves. The site includes ancient upland forests, one of the largest fishing and boating waters in Cook County, nearly 13 miles of paved trail, an elk pasture, and much more—making it one of the best-used natural areas in Illinois" (fpdcc.com).

Busse Woods had most certainly been part of our previous hiking grounds. We didn't go often, but we did go there occasionally.

Today, Dan wanted to take us hiking. I liked Busse Woods. They felt like they were far away from everything. You could almost get lost in there. It's a huge preserve and if you weren't careful, the forest could swallow you whole.

Justin got up, and we ate our French toast. We had orange juice and milk. Dan had coffee. It was pretty chilly. A high of only 68 today; it was about 52 right now. The air had that early autumn bite. Sharp, thin, almost metallic.

Dan wore his jeans, boot-like shoes, Superman T-shirt, and red Lyons Fire Department jacket.

I wore jeans, a tan V-neck sweater, a black Lyons EMT hoodie, and my Nike Cortez Navy Blue shoes.

Justin had on jeans and a red sweater with a medium-weight jacket and a pair of Velcro-closure tennis shoes. They were much easier to get on and off him than lace-ups. The sound of the Velcro ripping open in the quiet of the house felt louder than it should have.

9:10 A.M.

We left the house around 9:10. Dan had slung his army green crossbody bag over his shoulder—the same one he had carried that day in Saganashkee Slough when we stalked that couple through the woods.

What was he up to this time? That question never stopped burning in my mind.

I didn't see what he was packing. I could only guess. Maybe Itchy Brother was in there. Maybe the camouflage netting too.

By the time we pulled away, the clock was still showing 9:10, like it wanted to brand the moment in my head.

Busse Woods was less than 30 miles away. We took Ogden Avenue to Route 294, then cut over to I-290. At the Higgins Road/Route 72 exit, the road curved in that slow, deliberate loop. The kind that makes you wonder who designed it.

9:46 A.M.

We turned right on Higgins.

Once we entered Busse Wood via Higgins Road, we entered the entrance to Busse Forest North.

I have replayed this day in my head more times than I can count. The images were etched so sharply that they might as well be film stills. Using Google Earth, I have zoomed in on every single entrance to Busse Woods, matching them to the pictures burned into me. The aerial views left no doubt. This was the spot. And in all these decades, it has barely changed since 1982.

If you park your car in Busse Forest North, you can see a picnic table or two. If you look at both sides of the parking lot, the area is somewhat cleared but still pretty wooded.

I saw several motorcycles in the parking lot. Harley-Davidsons and the like. That is where he took us.

We walked along the parking lot area. There was a picnic table. We kept walking back, partially on a trail.

He handed me his watch.

"Remember how I showed you how to use a watch as a compass?" he asked.

"Yes," I said, knowing completely that I didn't grasp that idea fully—or at all.

We kept walking back into the woods. As we went deeper in, there was a pavilion set slightly back in the trees. We were hiking to the left of the pavilion.

There were people in the pavilion. Bikers. I'm not saying Hell's Angels or anything like that, but bikers. Leather vests, T-shirts, leather pants, etc. You get the idea.

Hyper Dan cautioned us not to make a noise.

I was thinking to myself, *He does know Justin is here with us, doesn't he?*

We were on the trail, still to the left of the people in the pavilion. They were having a good time.

Dan brought us slightly farther back into the woods. The bikers were still in my sight line.

He barely spoke a word. He pulled Itchy Brother from his bag. Laid it down on the ground after making a small clearing.

He was making his hand signals. Be quiet. Sit still. Stay here.

Wait a minute. Stay here? What the fuck is he doing?

He got down onto Itchy Brother with me. He unpacked a bag of Goldfish crackers and a few cans of Coke.

Whispering, barely audibly, he said, "See those people? They're very dangerous."

I was thinking, *Great. Wonderful. How nice of you to bring us to the middle of nowhere with "dangerous" people.*

But it gets worse.

Hyper Dan looked me square in the eyes—yes, my 11-year-old eyes—and said, "I need you to stay here with your brother."

All I could think was, *Fuck no!*

However, I didn't have the option of saying "fuck no."

He said that today, we were going to do a drill. A drill to see whether I could navigate my way back to the car.

"Remember that picnic table in the parking lot?"

"Yes," I said.

"I need you to stay here for one hour. Exactly one hour before you start to head back. Promise me that you'll wait one hour, then, using my watch as a compass like I taught you, you'll pack up the site and your brother and head back."

10:07 A.M.

And at that point, he was gone.

I saw the red Lyons Fire Department jacket walking away. Again. The same as 48 hours ago at Lincoln Park Zoo.

Except this time, I was alone in the woods with the *dangerous* bikers while I babysat my not-even-four-year-old brother.

There was no time to protest. No time for anything except to pray for the best.

THE BIKERS

Yes. The bikers. They were still there. They were almost close enough that I was shocked they didn't hear or see us or Hyper Dan. He moved like a ghost through the tree line.

He seemed like the persona that appeared when he was Hyper Dan. However, he was more focused. He didn't give me the chance to ask questions.

He had decided he was leaving us there, and that was it.

I was so fucking scared. I had all the same feelings pop up that I'd had at Lincoln Park Zoo two days ago.

There are no words that can explain how I felt left in the woods in charge of my little brother. Panicked, scared, helpless… Those don't even begin to describe my state.

FLASHBACK

We were on a walk. Not even hiking or anything. It was just us walking around. He said to me, "Have I ever taught you the rules of three?"

"Nope," I said.

He continued, "Here are the rules of three: three seconds of panic will kill you. Three minutes without oxygen will kill you. Three days without water will kill you. Three weeks without food will kill you."

Okay, not sure when I'll need those, but all right, *I thought.*

Well, the time for the rules of three was upon me. At least the first rule.

Three seconds of panic will kill you.

I took a deep breath. I looked at the watch.

10:20 A.M.

I sat with Justin, and I was trying not to say a word. The bikers were right there.

I wasn't worried about myself. I was worried about Justin. That he would let out a wail or something. He was very unpredictable.

We sat and sat.

10:32 A.M.

Justin started to get fidgety.

Shit. It has only been 25 minutes.

I tried using some hand signals that I learned from Hyper Dan, thinking that if Justin saw me not talking, he would do the same.

Not really. He took in a breath and was starting to make a noise, and...

I halfway stood up. I looked at him and I took a breath in, while at the same time making a funny face and putting my finger in front of my mouth, motioning *hush*.

I still don't know where that spur-of-the-moment idea came from, but it worked. Justin didn't make a peep. Not yet, at least.

While I was making that crazy face, I took it up a notch. I made a face like a goldfish. I think I was possibly looking at the goldfish crackers, and that is what came to mind.

Now, I was getting pissed. He fucking left us here in the woods. Alone. The reality was just sinking in.

I was thinking quietly to myself, *I swear to God, if something happens to one of us...*

10:48 A.M.

Are you fucking kidding me?

Adrenaline kicked in. I was so pissed that I wanted to scream. But I couldn't. There were *dangerous* bikers just a few steps away.

Justin sat down next to me. I looked at him, and I wanted to cry.

This kid has no idea, I thought silently.

And just like that. Justin laid his head down on me and fell asleep.

I watched him. Not even four years old. Sleeping on me on Itchy Brother. Left alone in the woods by our father.

I looked at him and I thought, *I have got to get us out of here.*

Justin was sleeping for a few minutes.

11:01 A.M.

I was sitting on Itchy Brother, Justin on me, and I started to think.

I was thinking that this is the most peace I have had, probably ever.

How did I find a sense of peace under these circumstances?
I don't know. Yet, there it was. Peace.

11:04 A.M.

It was like time was nearly standing still.

I sat there, keeping watch over my brother, watching and
listening to the bikers. Again, this crazy sense of peace.

The bikers were in the pavilion. Laughing. Talking.

I was finding it soothing to listen to their conversations and
laughter.

There were no harsh words. No yelling. No screaming. No
loaded pistols against anyone's head. Just people enjoying
their day.

To tell the truth, I was a bit envious. Envious of the freedom
they had. Freedom to jump on their bike at any time.
Freedom to enjoy the company of one another.

And, if I'm being even more truthful, I wanted to jump on
the back of one of their bikes and ride as far away from here
as possible. Ride as far away from Gage Avenue as possible.

11:17 AM. LATE.

*Fuck. I was enjoying my fantasy daydream so much that I
lost track of time. And here it comes. The panic.*

Three seconds of panic will kill you.

We had to start heading back to the picnic table in the lot at 11:07. I looked at the watch and gently nudged Justin awake.

He wasn't happy being woken up from his nap. He stood up and...

He took off running. Down the trail. The opposite way from where we needed to go. *You little shit.*

I took off behind him, scared he would start screaming.

I need to point out that in no way did I feel scared of the bikers.

My fear of the bikers as I chased Justin was that they would see us and do the unthinkable: ask questions.

Why are you boys out here in the woods alone? What kind of people leave their kids in the woods?

Just wait for about four decades and read this book, then you'll know.

That was my real fear. Questions.

We were to keep secrets.

I ran after Justin. I got up right behind him. He started to let out a wail. I put my hand over his mouth. He gave me a look like, *What the fuck?*

I picked him up and carried him under my left arm like a bag of groceries.

Oddly, he didn't make a peep. *I need to get back, pack everything up, and check the time. We have to move quickly.*

BACK AT ITCHY BROTHER

We got back to the site, and I started to fold up Itchy Brother. I shook it out. Gently, gently. I didn't want the bikers to see or hear us.

I was gathering everything up. I went to look down at the watch to check the time. The watch was gone. *FUCK.*

I must have dropped it when I had to apprehend Justin.

He's going to kill me. We're now late, and I don't have his watch.

I did what Dan had taught me. I retraced my steps.

Walk quietly with purpose. Always look up, down, to the left, to the right. Stick to the left.

I did just that. I went down the trail, still carrying Justin. I looked and looked.

There it was. This was just like the day I found the watch by First Avenue. There it was, in some tall grass. Oddly enough, to my left. Oddly enough, just like First Avenue.

11:27 A.M.

I still cannot believe that all of that happened in 10 minutes.

I carried Justin to get the cross-body bag, and we began walking down the trail.

Funny thing, though, I didn't even need to try to use the watch as a compass. He had left us about 10 yards off the trail that leads directly to the parking lot.

When we were walking out to the spot. It seemed like he was almost zigzagging or walking in a circle somewhat.

The truth was that this was a clean line, a straight path right back to the parking lot. Once again, my mind went to, *What the fuck is he up to?*

Poisons offer a quiet alternative to things that go *boom* in the night…

THE PARKING LOT

We walked back toward the parking lot, my feet crunching over the damp leaves scattered across the narrow trail. The air was thick with that unmistakable autumn scent: dry leaves, a faint trace of woodsmoke from somewhere far away, and the sharp, almost metallic bite of the cool air.

Something about the smell should have been comforting, familiar. It wasn't. Every breath felt like it carried a warning.

Something isn't right with this, I kept thinking, the words pounding in my head in rhythm with my footsteps.

The walk back felt different. Off, somehow. The trip into the woods had seemed endless, every step away from safety stretching the morning out like taffy. But now, the return felt shorter, wrong, like time itself had been altered. This wasn't right.

The trees broke, revealing the clearing ahead. I spotted the two picnic tables. Still there, unchanged. I scanned the lot. No Dan. No car. Just the same cluster of motorcycles, their chrome catching the pale light that filtered through the trees. The sight of them made my chest tighten.

I tried to convince myself to be grateful. At least the bikers hadn't seen us. That must have been a miracle. But the thought barely took root before it rotted into suspicion.

Wait. Where is he? Where is the car?

A cold shiver slid down my spine, settling deep in my stomach. *Fuck,* I muttered under my breath, panic rising. *We must have gotten back to a different parking lot.*

The confusion came first, sharp and dizzying. Then anger, hot and quick. And then fear. Real fear.

Shock anchored me where I stood. The motorcycles were here. They had been here when we arrived. This was the right parking lot. There was no mistake.

But where was Dan?

11:32 A.M.

Yes. This had most definitely been a much shorter trip back. My pulse quickened, my thoughts racing. *What the fuck is he up to? Where did he go? Why isn't he here waiting?*

I dropped down onto one of the picnic tables with Justin. The wooden seat was cold and damp beneath me. I could hear the bikers somewhere beyond the tree line, their voices and laughter drifting closer, muffled but unmistakable. Every sound made my muscles tighten.

I was getting pissed now. Really pissed.

What the fuck?

The words came out again, sharper this time. I froze when I heard the low growl of a car engine turning the corner. My eyes locked on the movement, my body tense.

The silver Buick station wagon rolled into view like nothing was wrong.

"Well, look who's back," I said aloud, my voice dripping with venom I didn't even try to hide.

11:34 A.M.

He had left at 10:07. I glanced at the watch again. It was now 11:34. He had been gone an hour and 27 minutes. No explanation. No apology. Just pulling up like this was any ordinary day.

Hyper Dan was back, grinning and jittery, the same giddy schoolgirl version of him I had seen before. And that, somehow, was worse than the silence.

He parked the car, stepped out without a word, and tossed the bag into the back of the station wagon.

I noticed something. Another crack in his façade. When he took the cross-body bag from me to put in the back, he seemed very, shall we say, guarded about the back of the station wagon.

He opened the back and stood where I couldn't see into the back. He tossed the bag in and quickly slammed the back.

What is he up to?

It was a small crack, but I had trained myself very well at this point to be hypervigilant about those small cracks. It was the small cracks that were always more dangerous than the larger cracks.

The crisp air filled my lungs, but the fall smell—the one I usually loved—felt wrong now. Like it wasn't just leaves decaying out there. Like something else was rotting too.

BACK IN THE BUICK

I was in the front seat. Justin was in the back. I wish I had sat back there. I could have done a quick turnaround and a peekaboo to see what he had back there. I was certain there was something I wasn't supposed to see.

I was still. So. Pissed.

I looked right over at him. He was singing along with some horrible old song that he had found on his oldies station, WJMK 104.3.

I made the decision to have a discussion with him in language and terms he would understand. "Can you tell me exactly what the fuck happened back there?" I demanded.

He almost crashed the car into a tree. I think he was shocked, but also somehow pleased at how I was attempting to grab the situation by the balls.

"Whoa, whoa, killer. What are you so upset about?" he replied.

I was thinking, *He wants to turn this around on me. Classic Dan behavior, whether Regular Dan, Evil Dan, Hyper Dan, or Deacon Dan. That is his M.O.*

"Are you fucking kidding me?" I was yelling at this point.

"Don't give me your stupid act. DUH, I don't know what you're talking about," I said. At this point, I wasn't even yelling anymore. I was screaming at him.

I was honestly waiting for a hand across the face or whatever part of me he could reach. I didn't care. What happened today was unacceptable.

It was at that moment that I became the parent. Not only looking out for Justin, but trying to rein Dan in.

This was the first time that I actually got visibly pissed off with him in my life. And I let him know about it.

That is why I can remember every second, every thought, every action, everything from that day so perfectly. This was a traumatic day for me, but also the day that I was done taking shit. And I let him know it.

"What's the problem? I told you I was testing you to see if you could make it back to the car," he said.

"You left us. Alone. In the woods. With the 'dangerous' bikers only feet away from us. I don't know. Why don't you tell me what the problem is? And to top it off, you were gone when we got back!" I yelled.

"Well, aren't we sensitive today. Are you getting your period today, young lady?" He was giggling. Schoolgirl behavior.

"Look," he said. I always knew when he said "look" that he was about to get serious.

"I had some errands to run while you were in the woods. I knew you would get back all right and everything would be okay," he said very quietly.

"Errands? What errands?" I questioned him. "We don't even live out here."

"Okay, smartass. I'm aware that we don't live out here, but even though we don't live out here, they still have stores. You are aware of that, right?" His tone was biting.

He was trying to knock me off target. I held firm.

Stores. What stores? I was thinking.

"Yes. I'm aware of that. That isn't an excuse for leaving your kids in the woods. Alone. With the bikers."

He got quiet. I was ready. *Bring it, Hyper Dan or whoever you are right now.* I was thinking. And… nothing.

I had shut him down. At least temporarily.

He didn't apologize or acknowledge what he had done. He never did. He remained quiet. Kept driving.

I was looking out the window. We were still in what appeared to be kind of a wooded area.

The way back home from Busse Woods would be the reverse of the way we came out here, 99% highway. This wasn't the highway.

I couldn't even deal with him at this point. I sat quietly. He sat quietly. After a few moments of glorious silence, he spoke.

"I don't know about you boys, but I'm starving."

Finally, something we could agree on.

After we had reached our quiet resolution to agree to disagree, I started to calm down.

ON THE ROAD AGAIN

Dan was taking back roads. That much was for sure. Where we were going was another question. We got to a busy intersection and turned left. This didn't look familiar to me at all.

We drove for barely a minute, and to my right, I saw Santa's Village.

Santa's Village is an amusement park in East Dundee, Illinois. We had gone there many, many times. Though not far from Busse Woods, Santa's Village was in the complete opposite direction from Lyons.

I remembered the other times we had been to Santa's Village; we had eaten at this cool and fun Western-looking restaurant. I was hoping that was where we were heading.

He put on his left turn signal. Yes. We were going to Aunt Kate Fisher's Boardin' House. As he turned left into the parking lot, another car entered the road and blew its horn at him. He exploded. He turned the car around like he was going to chase them down.

"You fuckin' cocksucker. If I didn't have my goddamn kids in the car, I'd bash your fuckin' brains in. If you had any."

Shit, here we go. Evil Dan is back.

He did chase them. He followed the car down to the next light. They made it through. He didn't. I'm certain that they wanted to avoid this crazy man. That was probably the right decision.

Now what? He popped a U-turn at the light, and we headed back once again to Aunt Kate Fisher's Boardin' House.

Same drill as before. We were turning left. We go into the parking lot, and what?

It was closed. I don't know if the restaurant was closed permanently or just for the day. I cannot say.

Dan parked the car anyway. He got out, went up to the restaurant, and then walked around to the back of the building.

Okay. Now was my chance. I needed to investigate what was in the back that he was hiding from me. How?

Do I get out and sneak a peek? Or do I get into the back under the guise of checking on Justin? I chose the latter. Safer choice.

I jumped in the back. Justin started yelling at me, "Go back front." This little asshole that I had just kept alive in the woods was giving me shit.

I took a quick glimpse into the back of the wagon.

THE RETURN OF DAN

ABORT. ABORT.

Instead of being totally obvious by jumping back up front, I pretended like I was checking Justin's seat. Anything to not look suspicious.

The only things that I saw in the back were…

The khaki green cross-body and two cardboard boxes. In fact, one of the cardboard boxes was the box I had seen in the lair within the lair on my previous expedition.

Again, I saw the boxes so quickly. This time, I could make out some faint letters in faded black. That was it. It was pretty much illegible in the quick flash of time that my eyes were on it.

"Sorry, boys, it looks like Aunt Kate's is closed."

I jumped back in the front seat. He didn't question what I was doing in the back. I believe he saw me pretending to tend to Justin.

He got into the driver's seat and off we went. I knew this area a little bit because we had been to Santa's Village and Aunt Kate's enough times in the past.

He pulled out and turned right. He went down to the stoplight where he had previously chased the offensive driver who had the nerve to blow the horn at him.

I knew this wasn't the right way home. This was the way we had come into East Dundee. He did another U-turn at the light and headed back down Dundee Avenue.

We took Dundee Avenue. I knew exactly where we were now. I was thinking that he would head up to I-90 and we would trek back to 290 and then go the reverse way that we had gone to Busse.

As we approached the intersection at Dundee Ave to merge onto I-90, he stopped. Swerved the car to the right.

"Hey, boys! There is a Howard Johnson's. They serve pancakes twenty-four hours a day. Anyone up for pancakes?!"

HOWARD JOHNSON'S

He parked the car in the lot at Howard Johnson's. We walked in. It was now about 12:30. Justin was getting cranky because he was hungry. The stress of the hike of doom had worn me out. It's funny how the body reacts to stress. I could have walked one hundred miles while we were abandoned in the woods. Now I had nothing left. I felt my resistance dwindling.

The moment we stepped inside, the air hit me—thick with the smell of butter melting on hot griddles. Pancakes, bacon, fried potatoes. Sweet syrup mixed with scorched coffee. The scent clung to my clothes, seeped into my skin. Plates clattered against one another in the background. Silverware scraped on ceramic. Voices hummed low, drowned out by the hiss of the kitchen.

We got in Howard Johnson's, and the hostess said, "Table for three, gentlemen?"

"Gentlemen? You have no idea who you're dealing with," he said with his Cheshire-Cat-like smirk.

She sat us at a booth. The vinyl stuck slightly to my legs when I slid in. A few minutes later, the waitress came over.

Dan ordered for us all. "Coffee for me and OJ for my boys."

"I'd also like two orders of your best pancakes and a side order of bacon. Oh yeah. I need an extra plate or two and all the napkins you can spare. This little fucker is messy."

The waitress giggled at him.

"One more thing. Can we get some peanut butter too? My kids like peanut butter on their pancakes."

"Okie dokie. Comin' right up, sir."

The smell grew heavier as plates passed by our table. Pancakes stacked high. Bacon curling on the edges. Syrup dripping slow like amber. The diner air felt thick, heavy, suffocating.

At this point, I was dizzy from watching so many versions of Dan over the past several hours.

We sat quietly for a few minutes. Dan looked at his wrist. Fuck. His watch. I knew I had put it under the seat in the car.

"Shit. I feel naked without my watch. You didn't lose it, did you?" he said with a shit-eating grin on his face.

"No. I put it under my seat in the car." Oh, if he had only known that it had been temporarily lost.

"I'm going out to get it. Under your seat, right?"

I nodded yes.

He was gone for a very brief few minutes. Four at the most. He came back and sat at the table. "Ah. Much better now." He had his watch back on.

Silence. Again.

A few minutes later, the pancakes arrived. Uneventful.

This moment in time is one of those moments where nothing eventful happens, but for some reason, you hold onto it.

I watched him put on the butter, a little peanut butter, then douse the pancakes with syrup. Completely uneventful.

He cut some pancakes up for Justin and put them on a plate for him. Justin attempted to eat them himself. That was going to be a disaster. Dan intervened and fed Justin.

Again, completely uneventful.

I did the same with my pancakes. I vividly remember grabbing the syrup container. It was very sticky as I poured it over my pancakes. The glass neck of the bottle felt tacky against my palm. My fingers clung to it. The syrup ran slowly, thick, golden brown, pooling across the butter and peanut butter that melted into the hot surface. The smell rose up. Sweet. Heavy. Overpowering.

The waiters and waitresses slid plates across other tables. Forks clinked. Knives scraped. A steady chorus of voices droned around us, muffled by distance yet pressing close, mixing with the hiss of grease from the kitchen. I could hear the faint crackle of bacon still sizzling on some unseen skillet. The air was a storm of scents. Pancakes, fried potatoes, sausage fat, bitter coffee.

Sweetness folded into salt.

We sat as a father and his two sons eating pancakes.

Completely uneventful, but I have that day etched into the fabric of my being. The sights, the sounds, the terror mixed with the sweetness and saltiness of Howard Johnson's.

We wrapped up with the pancakes. Dan paid at the register with cash. We headed out the door. Justin was nearly asleep. Dan carried him.

When we left, I headed back to where the car was parked. As I turned, Dan grabbed my hoodie. "Over here, genius."

It seemed like I was going the wrong way. "No. The car is over here," I proclaimed.

"Maybe you're not as observant as you think you are."

I knew with every fiber of my being that the car was parked where I was headed. We got to the car.

Yes. This was our car.

No. This was most definitely not where we had parked it.

Why did he move the car? These words ran through my head.

I absolutely had no strength to argue with him. My body was drained. My will was gone. The fight had been stripped out of me. The car was where the car was. He had made it so. I let it go.

BACK TO LYONS

As I depicted earlier, the route back to Lyons was getting on 90. Taking 90 to 290. On to 294 to Ogden. Ogden back to Gage.

As we drove down 290, I could see Busse Woods to my left, where we had our earlier hike of doom. To my right stood Woodfield Mall. The two places were only separated by a few lanes of highway. On one side, the ancient upland woods. On the other, a modern mega-mall.

By the time we got back to Gage Avenue, Justin was fully asleep. I was ready for a nap. Dan lovingly carried Justin up the walkway. I trailed behind.

To the casual observer, one would think, *Look how sweet that is. A man coming back home from hiking with his sons. Carrying the little one.*

The picture-perfect moment of fatherhood. The kind of scene that neighbors glance at through curtains and smile, never knowing the truth.

Evil Dan was back at this time, though. He turned to me, eyes as black as coal. As we approached the front stairs, he very calmly turned to me. Still carrying Justin, asleep.

"If you ever tell anyone about the things that went down today, I'll kill you. I'll kill your mother. I'll kill your brother and sister. Understood?"

The sweetness shattered into shit. The warm image of a father carrying his son became a mask hiding the blackest threat I had ever heard up to this point in my life.

This was the last time I ever went anywhere with my father without another adult present.

"The safest way to test poisons, for you... is to put it in an enemy's medicine. If you have access to his bathroom, look for capsules...

I saw the capsule trick on *Ironside*.

Clever."

(*The Poor Man's James Bond*, Vol.1. p. 53)

Poisons offer a quiet alternative to things that go *boom* in the night…

SECTION FOUR

CHAPTER SIX: THE AFTERMATH

TUESDAY, SEPTEMBER 28, 1982

I woke up for school around 7:30. I was worn out from the previous day. My body ached, my head felt heavy, and I thought maybe a cold was coming on. Either way, there was no choice. Time to get ready for school.

Dan was gone. Nowhere to be seen. Maybe he was at Electro-Motive. Maybe at the police department. Maybe at the firehouse. Or maybe just out doing whatever the hell he felt like doing.

Maybe running some more errands to stores that we didn't live near. I voted for the last one.

He had taken the powder blue Vega.

I moved through my morning as usual and went to school. Nothing about the rest of that day stood out for me. Uneventful, at least in my own orbit.

But in other news, the world outside my small circle was shifting.

ELGIN, ILLINOIS

Deputy Joseph Chavez pulled into the parking lot of the Howard Johnson's Motor Lodge and Restaurant in Elgin, Illinois. It was the early morning hours of Tuesday, September 28, 1982. His shift for the Kane County Sheriff's Department had just ended. He was working the midnight to 8:00 a.m. rotation, and like many nights, this all-night diner was the natural stop for breakfast. A moment later, Deputy Al Swanson arrived and parked beside him.

At 2:32 a.m., both men stepped from their vehicles and started toward the entrance of the restaurant. The fluorescent lights over the parking lot caught something odd. Two cardboard boxes left on the pavement, resting near the grass median that divided the restaurant's parking lot from Route 25. The boxes stood out, unattended, strangely positioned. As Chavez and Swanson approached, the stenciled markings became clear. The words "EXTRA STRENGTH TYLENOL CAPSULES" were stamped in faded black lettering across the right side of each box. The opposite side bore the manufacturer's name, McNEIL, with the printed description: twelve six-packs of 50-count bottles of Extra Strength Tylenol capsules.

One of the boxes had already been opened. Inside sat nearly two dozen Tylenol bottles. Two of them had been pried open. Scattered across the pavement were hundreds of capsule halves. Red and white, stamped with the familiar 500 mg dosage mark of Extra Strength Tylenol. Between the boxes lay something worse: a mound of loose white powder, a pile so conspicuous it looked as if it had been dumped straight out of the capsules.

"It looked like hundreds of capsules had been emptied," Chavez would later recall. "We looked at them and found a couple of capsules that had been put back together."

The deputies bent down, curious but unconcerned. Chavez picked up a few capsules, turned them over in his hand, then tossed them back onto the ground. Swanson did the same, even stooping to pinch some of the powder between his fingers. They speculated. Maybe drug dealers had tampered with the bottles, emptied the acetaminophen, planning to refill the capsules with cocaine. That would explain the pile, the sloppy scattering. But something did not sit right. The reassembled capsules were mismatched. The 500 mg markings on the halves did not line up correctly.

Still, the two men brushed it off. They left the open boxes exactly where they had been found. The strange debris of Tylenol littered the lot behind them as they stepped inside the restaurant, slid into a booth, and ordered breakfast.

As they ate, Chavez began to feel it. A headache came first, dull and pounding. Then a burning sensation, a rash breaking out along his arm, swelling beneath the skin, and pain radiating upward. Swanson soon followed, but worse. Minutes after leaving the restaurant, he pulled his squad car to the side of the road, overcome. He vomited violently. His head spun with dizziness. The suddenness was shocking. Both deputies were showing symptoms of cyanide poisoning.

Headache, vomiting, disorientation, and dizziness. Cyanide could kill through ingestion, but also by touch. The white powder scattered across the parking lot may already have entered their systems.

Despite the sickness, neither man connected what had just happened to the capsules. They drove off, leaving the boxes behind in the Howard Johnson's lot at the intersection of Route 25 and Interstate 90. About 38 miles northwest of Chicago. The two boxes remained where they had been left, evidence of something far more sinister than the deputies realized at that moment.

Citation:

Schulz, H. (2016, September 29). "Cyanide-Laced Tylenol Murder: Anniversary of Significant Unsolved Murder Case in Arlington Heights and Nation." Arlington Cardinal. https://www.arlingtoncardinal.com/2016/09/cyanide-laced-tylenol-murder- anniversary-of-significant-unsolved-murder-case-in-arlington-heights-and-nation/

WEDNESDAY, SEPTEMBER 29, 1982
SUNRISE: 6:45 A.M.
SUNSET: 6:36 P.M.

I woke up for school around 7:30. The weight of the last few days still clung to me. I felt slow, drained, as if sickness had started creeping into my bones. My throat scratched faintly. My body told me to stay in bed. Our weather had been like a yo-yo. Today was going to be a high of 85. This wasn't normal. None of this was normal. But school waited. The world expected me to move, even when every part of me wanted stillness.

Dan was gone. Again. The powder blue Vega was missing from the drive. His whereabouts were a mystery. I hadn't seen him in a few days.

Good.

He could have been at Electro-Motive. He could have been with the police. He could have been at the firehouse. Or more likely, he could have been exactly where he pleased, untethered, unaccountable. He always moved as though rules belonged to everyone else.

So, I carried on. I got dressed. I dragged myself forward, head heavy, body reluctant. Another morning in a string of mornings that felt the same. I had no way of knowing how close death was hovering that day, that hour, that moment.

Because as I stumbled into my routine, another child, 12 years old, just one year older than me, was also waking up. Just 19 miles away.

ELK GROVE VILLAGE, ILLINOIS – MARY KELLERMAN

Mary Kellerman woke in her room around the same hour I did. Her voice carried the strain of a sore throat. Her chest rattled with a cough. A child's small complaint, nothing extraordinary. Her father, Dennis, rose from his bed, walked the hall, and checked on her. He told her to stay home from school to rest. It sounded like mercy. Like loving care.

He stepped into the bathroom, opened the cabinet, and pulled down the same kind of bottle that sat in countless homes across America. Extra Strength Tylenol. A brand so ordinary, so trusted, that the red-and-white capsules inside looked like comfort. The night before, Mary's mother, Jeanna, had purchased the bottle at Jewel-Osco. Freshly stocked shelves. A simple act. A mother's errand.

Dennis returned to Mary's bedside. He gave her a single capsule. He believed he was helping his daughter. He thought he was easing her pain, the way any parent would.

I shouldered my backpack and left for school. I felt sluggish, my head buzzing, but I walked out the door anyway. I walked into an ordinary day.

Mary Kellerman swallowed her capsule. Then silence began to close around her.

Dennis returned to his own bed, only to hear the bathroom door shut, then a sudden crash. He rushed down the hallway, calling her name through the door. "Mary, are you okay?" No answer. He asked again. Louder this time. Still no answer. He opened the door.

There on the bathroom floor lay his daughter.

Mary was in full cardiac arrest. Her body had betrayed her within minutes of swallowing what she believed was medicine.

Paramedics arrived.

They worked on the bathroom floor. They worked in the ambulance.

They worked at Alexian Brothers Medical Center.

Nothing brought her back. At 10:00 a.m., Mary Kellerman was pronounced dead. Doctors at that moment could only mutter vague guesses. Aneurysm, heart attack. Blind to the truth seeping in like poison.

I sat in a classroom at Robinson, doing pre-algebra with Ms. Bernard.

Mary's family was watching the unthinkable unfold.

I went through a school day that was nothing but ordinary.

Mary Kellerman never made it to school. Ever again.

The coin had been tossed. Heads—I lived. Tails—Mary Kellerman didn't.

MARY KELLERMAN'S BOTTLE

Mary's mother, Jeanna Kellerman, purchased a 50-count bottle of Extra Strength Tylenol from a Jewel Food Store in Elk Grove Village around 4:00 p.m. on Sept. 28, 1982. A later examination of the bottle revealed that it contained 51 extra strength capsules, six of which contained cyanide.

ARLINGTON HEIGHTS, ILLINOIS – ADAM JANUS WEDNESDAY, SEPTEMBER 29, 1982

I went through the motions of school that day. In biology, we dissected frogs. These were my friends from American Science & Surplus, the formaldehyde emitting a sweet and strange odor. My heart still ached for them. My body sat at a desk, but my mind drifted. Nothing remarkable. Nothing felt off at school. By all accounts, it was still an ordinary Wednesday.

But not far away, death was already working its way into homes.

Adam Janus was just 27, a postal worker in Elk Grove Village. A man who had crossed oceans for a better life, leaving Poland in 1970, then returning five years later to marry his sweetheart, Teresa. Together, they carved out a beautiful life in Arlington Heights. They bought a small home. They had a steady rhythm of days. On that Wednesday, Adam had taken the day off. Feeling a bit sick. A break from work. Just another day on the calendar.

Later that morning, Adam drove to the Jewel-Osco on Vail Avenue. He walked the aisles, choosing a steak for dinner, flowers for his wife, and, almost as an afterthought, a bottle of Extra Strength Tylenol. Nothing sinister in the act. Just a husband running errands.

He returned home. Lunch with Teresa. Simple. Ordinary. Then he swallowed two capsules from the bottle he had just purchased. Within minutes, the ordinary twisted into horror. He told Teresa he didn't feel well. He retreated to the bedroom to lie down.

While I sat watching a film strip in Mrs. Jones's classroom. Adam collapsed in his home. Teresa found him minutes later. Unconscious, convulsing. She called for help.

Paramedics arrived around 2:00 p.m. They found Adam unconscious, his breathing labored, blood pressure collapsing, pupils fixed and dilated. Nothing they tried worked. They rushed him to Northwest Community Hospital, but at 3:15 p.m., Adam Janus was pronounced dead. At that same moment, my final school bell rang at Robinson.

Doctors gathered Adam's family. His wife, his parents, his brother Stanley, and Stanley's wife Theresa. Dr. Thomas Kim, the ICU director, spoke plainly: "Nothing seemed to help. He suffered sudden death without warning. It was most unusual."

As I meandered through another school day, Adam's life was being cut short by the same capsules that had looked so harmless, so trusted. He had bought dinner, flowers, and Tylenol. He carried them home in a Brown Jewel 50th Anniversary paper bag. By nightfall, only the steak and the flowers remained untouched.

ARLINGTON HEIGHTS, ILLINOIS PART TWO – STANLEY JANUS THERESA JANUS WEDNESDAY, SEPTEMBER 29, 1982

Adam Janus's 24-year-old brother Stanley, and Stanley's 19-year-old wife, also named Theresa, left Northwest Community Hospital late Wednesday afternoon. They had just stood with Adam's widow Teresa, watching as his body was pronounced beyond saving. The three of them drove back to Arlington Heights. Back to Adam's house. Back to the kitchen, where the bottle of Extra Strength Tylenol still sat on the counter, quiet, ordinary, and lethal.

The grief hung thick. Their eyes were red from crying. Their heads were pounding with tension. Stanley rubbed at his temples. His wife, Theresa, complained of the same. Headaches, they said, most certainly from the exhaustion and sadness of the day. Stanley reached for the Tylenol. He shook out two red-and-white capsules into his palm and swallowed them without hesitation. The same capsules that had ended his brother's life just hours earlier although, of course, he had no idea.

Theresa picked up the phone. She dialed her parents. She had to deliver the news of her brother-in-law's death. She hung up. She wiped her eyes. She reached for the same bottle. She shook out two capsules, tilted her head back, and swallowed. Another innocent act. Another nail hammered down into fate's coffin.

Stanley carried the bottle into the bathroom and placed it in the medicine cabinet. He returned to the kitchen. Lit a cigarette. Tried to steady himself. He never made it outside. He collapsed instead, his body seizing in violent convulsions.

Panic set in. Theresa called the Arlington Heights Fire Department at 6:00 p.m. For the second time that day, they rushed to the Janus house. They worked on Stanley in the kitchen, trying to breathe life back into a man who had unknowingly swallowed death.

Meanwhile, back in Lyons, Dan had finally returned. He made steaks on the grill. Where had he been? I had barely seen him the last two days.

We ate our dinner.

We were now getting ready to leave for Wednesday night Bible study.

Odd. We didn't usually go to church on Wednesday unless Grandma was here.

In Arlington Heights, death had more business inside the Janus house.

Theresa watched her husband's body being fought over by strangers in uniforms. She called her parents again. She tried to explain that Stanley was about to be taken to the hospital. Her voice cracked with terror. Then, mid-sentence, she collapsed onto the living room floor.

Two bodies down within minutes.

Dr. Thomas Kim, the same doctor who had worked on Adam earlier that day, was about to leave Northwest Community Hospital when the call came in. Adam's brother and sister-in-law were on their way in, both of them were in full cardiac arrest. Kim removed his jacket. He waited. He already knew the futility of the fight.

Paramedics tried, just as they had hours earlier. They worked on Stanley. They worked on Theresa. Their bodies followed the exact same trajectory as Adam's. Convulsions, heart failure, collapse. Theresa was briefly revived. Her heart was forced back into rhythm, but her brain was gone. Machines could make her chest rise and fall, but nothing could bring her back.

Dr. Kim went through his mental checklist, searching for answers. The symptoms were too violent, too sudden, too precise to be a coincidence. He ordered calls to poison control. The Rocky Mountain Poison Center responded. Dr. John Sullivan listened to the details, then cut through the fog. It was cyanide. Nothing else fit.

That night, the truth surfaced. Poison had turned taking an ordinary medicine into a death sentence.

Helen Jensen, a public health nurse in Arlington Heights, had just sat down to a late dinner when her phone rang. Northwest Community Hospital needed her immediately. Something strange was happening, they said. She left her half-eaten plate and drove into the chaos.

By the time she arrived, the staff was already buzzing in anxious whispers, trying to comprehend how a trusted bottle of Tylenol had wiped out three members of a single family in less than 24 hours.

ADAM, STANLEY, AND THERESA JANUS'S BOTTLE

Adam Janus had purchased a 50-count bottle of Extra Strength Tylenol from a Jewel Food Store in Arlington Heights around 11:00 a.m. on Sept. 29, 1982. A later examination of the bottle revealed that it contained 44 extra strength capsules, four of which contained cyanide.

OSCO DRUG BOTTLES

The U.S. Food and Drug Administration discovered two contaminated 50-count bottles of Extra Strength Tylenol at an Osco Drug inside Woodfield Mall in Schaumburg on Sept. 30, 1982. An examination of the bottle revealed that it contained 50 extra strength capsules, 14 of which contained cyanide.

BUSSE WOODS TIMELINE

If there is any doubt about this timeline, I ask you to step back for a moment. Open your mind's eye and look down from above. See Busse Woods from the air—an endless sprawl of trees and water, the arteries of darkened roads threading around its body. What appears tranquil from above, however, becomes far more sinister when you realize what can be hidden there, what can be done unseen.

I have constructed multiple routes my father may have taken out of Busse Woods. I tested them all. I ran them against one another. Each came up with the same conclusion. The time always matches. The forest roads and the city streets bend to the same cold mathematics, no matter which direction you try to escape. My timings are built on modern maps. Google's clockwork precision is in 2025, but the dread behind them belongs completely to 1982.

I'm certain, having known how my father's mind worked, that he chose this particular path. This sequence of turns and choices. He wasn't a man of improvisation in these matters. He was deliberate, precise, and calculating. In his words, he was a trained assassin. When he set something into motion, the result was never an accident.

Dan left Justin and me in Busse Woods at 10:07 a.m. He vanished into the green labyrinth, and with each passing minute, the weight of his absence pressed harder against the air. He didn't return until 11:34 a.m., an absence that stretched for one hour and 27 minutes. A window of time that yawns wide with malice and premeditation.

In those 87 minutes, the forest itself seemed to hold its breath. And when he returned, it wasn't relief that met us, but a gnawing realization. Something had been set in motion that could never be undone.

THE ROUTES AND THE WINDOW OF TIME

From Busse Woods North, the path to Woodfield Mall was a short one, 2.6 miles. No more than five minutes. Two tainted bottles were turned in from the Osco Drug at Woodfield Mall, a store that sat unsuspecting beneath the hum of fluorescent lights, never knowing that death had already been slipped onto its shelves. Dan would have placed these boxes toward the front of the others on the shelf.

From Woodfield Mall, the drive to the Jewel on Vail Avenue in Arlington Heights stretched five miles, 14 minutes at most. The kind of distance one could cover without drawing notice, without raising suspicion. Dan would have placed these boxes toward the front of the others on the shelf.

From Arlington Heights to the Jewel in Elk Grove Village was 6.2 miles, 16 minutes at most. Another ordinary drive, another errand disguised as routine. Dan would have placed these boxes toward the front of the others on the shelf.

And then, from Elk Grove Village back to Busse Forest North, just 2.9 miles. Seven minutes. The circle closed, and the route was complete.

All told, the driving alone required about 42 minutes. Yet Dan was gone for 87 minutes. That left 45 long minutes. Three-quarters of an hour unaccounted for, time enough to slip unnoticed through each location. Time enough to move among the aisles like a shadow, leaving behind death wrapped in the disguise of medicine. If divided evenly, that gave him 15 minutes per store. More than enough time for someone who thrived on efficiency, who wasted nothing, not even a glance.

And consider the detail that chills me most. He was wearing his red Lyons Fire Department jacket that day. Who would question a fireman? Who would even glance twice at a man who carried himself with the authority of safety and rescue? In truth, it was the perfect camouflage, a mask that made him untouchable.

There are things about that day that cannot be dismissed. Busse Woods wasn't chosen by accident. It was deliberate, a stage he had long prepared in his mind. Here, among the trees and the stillness, he left his most haunting imprint. It was less an act of impulse than a ritual, carried out with the precision of someone who had been waiting for the calendar to turn, marking time until the right moment arrived.

Busse was his ground zero. I have no doubt. For him, it wasn't merely about destruction. It was about remembrance. For everyone else, it was horror unfolding in silence. He wasn't simply sick. He was bound to a rhythm of violence, tethered to the woods, the lake, and the ghosts of his past. That is all I can say about this morbid anniversary at this time.

THE EFFICIENCY OF THE PLAN

The more I study these routes, the more I'm struck by his efficiency. He never needed the full 15 minutes per location. That was far too generous for him. Dan worked quickly, with the precision of someone who had rehearsed the moves in his mind long before he ever set foot in those stores. Every second had a purpose. Every action was pared down to its cruelest efficiency.

And if there were bottles that were found but never disclosed? I know in my bones they would have been planted close to Busse Woods. He would have kept them near the perimeter, within reach of the forest's cover. Woodfield Mall itself lay just across the highway from Busse, practically within sight. The Jewel on Vail Avenue in Arlington Heights fell within the orbit of his chosen ground. The Jewel in Elk Grove Village, again, pressed close to Busse.

Patterns emerge when you stare long enough. He clung to the edge of Busse like a predator circling its territory. What kept him there?

We may never know. But what we do know is enough. These weren't random scatterings of poison. They were deliberate placements, calculated with chilling intent. Bombs, each one. And he planted them with the calm assurance of a man who knew no one would stop him. No one ever did.

Poisons offer a quiet alternative to things that go *boom* in the night…

WINFIELD, ILLINOIS – MARY "LYNN" REINER
SEPTEMBER 29, 1982

At nearly the same moment Adam's life ended at 3:15 p.m. on September 29, 1982, 27-year-old Mary "Lynn" Reiner was completing an errand of her own. Just one day out of the hospital after giving birth to her son, she stopped at Frank's Finer Foods in Winfield. She purchased a bottle of Regular Strength Tylenol, then drove home to her family— her newborn Joshua, her husband Ed, her older children, and her mother-in-law, who was helping with the little ones.

It should have been a quiet homecoming, a young mother easing back into her life. Instead, the house soon filled with terror. Lynn sat down in the living room and pulled out two Extra Strength Tylenol capsules. She swallowed them without hesitation. Within minutes, nausea swept over her, and she told her mother-in-law she wasn't feeling well. She tried to rise, moving toward the kitchen, but dizziness overtook her. She collapsed into a chair, her breath faltering.

Chaos erupted. Ed arrived home as Lynn's condition worsened. Her body was failing before their eyes. His mother shouted for him to call an ambulance. Ed's hands trembled as he fumbled with the phone. He dropped the receiver, his panic only feeding the frenzy of the moment. When he finally placed the call, Lynn's body gave way. She collapsed to the floor in full convulsions.

The police and paramedics arrived within minutes, but they were powerless. Lynn was rushed to Central DuPage Hospital, where doctors struggled to keep her alive. For her eight-year-old daughter Michelle, the memory never faded. She would forever remember the sounds: her mother hitting the floor, gasping for air, the chaos of voices shouting commands as she stood frozen at the edge of the scene.

Sirens blared as her mother was carried away, swallowed by the night.

There has always been a bit of mystery around Mary Reiner's Tylenol purchase.

The bottle purchased at Frank's Finer Foods was, by all accounts, a bottle of Regular Strength Tylenol. Placed in the bottle were, I believe, eight Extra Strength Tylenol capsules. It's believed that Mary took two. The original eight minus the two that she took would bring us to the remaining six.

Where did these extra strength capsules come from? The prevailing theory is that they were provided by Central DuPage Hospital in a blister pack after the birth of Joshua. With all due respect, I have another theory.

At the time of the murders, Tylenol had been marketing a free, small sample bottle of Extra Strength Tylenol. Eight capsules, to be exact. Some of these free samples were packaged with Regular Strength Tylenol.

It could have been possible that Mary Reiner received one of these free sample bottles with her Regular Strength Tylenol purchase. It's also entirely possible that Mary had poured the contents into the bottle of Regular Strength Tylenol.

I have worked and reworked this theory to the point of questioning random people if they purchased this combo deal, would they have poured the Extra Strength Tylenol into the Regular Strength Tylenol bottle? The answer has been overwhelmingly "yes."

WINFIELD TIMELINE

On September 26, 1982, my family gathered at Mary Ann and Jimmy's house in Warrenville. Their home sat less than two miles from Frank's Finer Foods in Winfield, a place that now takes on a sinister weight when viewed through the lens of what would soon follow.

That afternoon, my father and his brother left on what they called a beer run. Dan wore his red Lyons Fire Department jacket. It was no ordinary errand. Nearly two hours passed before they returned. In that expanse of time, a veil of uncertainty descends. What else was done, where else was traveled, and what might have been left behind? All once again under the guise of safety. A fireman and his brother out running an errand. Nothing to see here.

The geography alone raises the hair on the back of the neck. That house, that store, that window of absence—all of it together paints a chilling picture. The opportunity was there, and the hours stretched long enough for more than just beer to have been collected. Where else was a bomb planted in that area? Dan would have placed this box somewhere in the middle of the other boxes.

MARY "LYNN" REINER'S BOTTLE

Mary "Lynn" Reiner purchased a 50-count bottle of Regular Strength Tylenol from a Frank's Finer Foods store in Winfield around 3:00 p.m. on Sept. 29, 1982. A later examination of the bottle revealed that it contained 41 regular Tylenol capsules and six extra strength capsules. Four of the extra strength capsules contained cyanide.

Another Frank's Finer Foods **Bottle**

A DuPage County woman purchased a 50-count bottle of Extra Strength Tylenol from a Frank's Finer Foods in Wheaton around 10:30 a.m. on Sept. 29, 1982. After hearing the warnings about Tylenol, the woman turned the bottle in to the Wheaton Police Department. An examination of the bottle revealed that it contained 50 extra strength capsules, seven of which contained cyanide. Dan and Randy had been gone for nearly two hours.

Poisons offer a quiet alternative to things that go *boom* in the night…

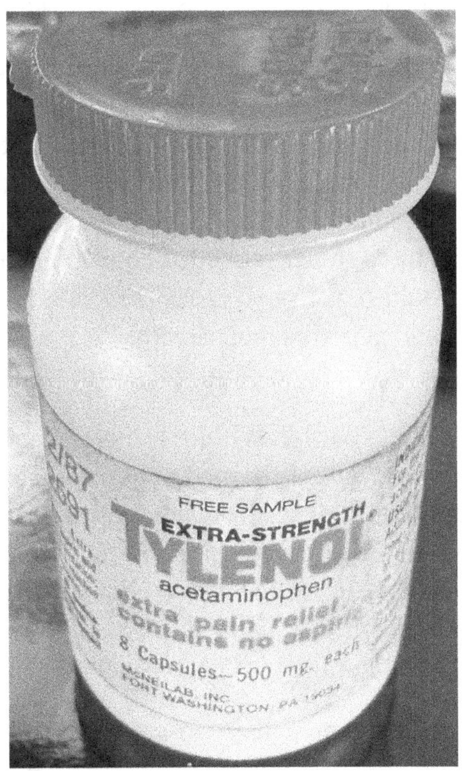

Extra-Strength Tylenol sample bottle with a comparable expiration date to the reported batch: recovered from my father's personal belongings after his death. Consistent in labeling, format, and era with products in circulation during the early 1980s. Credit: Courtesy of Joseph Cibelli (personal collection).

SEPTEMBER 29, 1982 — MARY MCFARLAND ELMHURST/LOMBARD

Not long after Mary "Lynn" Reiner collapsed and was rushed into Central DuPage Hospital around 5:00 p.m., another life was quietly ticking down 10 miles to the east, in Lombard. Thirty-one-year-old Mary McFarland was finishing her shift at the Bell Phone Center inside Yorktown Mall. The divorced mother of two had been battling a relentless headache all day. She reached into her purse, searching for the small bottle that promised relief: Extra Strength Tylenol capsules.

The capsules had come from the Woolworth store located in that very mall. The night before, Mary had stopped there after work, purchasing a fresh 50-count bottle of Extra Strength Tylenol. At home, she had carefully transferred 17 of the capsules into a smaller container. She used an old Dristan bottle to keep them in her purse for convenience, a habit so ordinary it would never have raised suspicion. By the next evening, she had already taken several. In the breakroom of her workplace, weary from pain, she swallowed two more.

The effect came swiftly. Within minutes, unease spread through her body. Nausea churned in her stomach. Dizziness clouded her vision. She rose from her seat. staggering toward a table where her co-workers sat. Her voice trembled as she tried to explain, "I don't feel good, guys." Then, with no warning, her body gave way. She collapsed forward, striking the table before slumping into unconsciousness.

Panic seized the room. Her co-workers rushed to her side, calling for help. Paramedics soon arrived. Mary was transported to Good Samaritan Hospital in Downers Grove. By 7:20 p.m., she was under medical care, but doctors struggled to determine what had struck her down so violently. To them, it looked like a catastrophic medical event. An aneurysm, perhaps, or a sudden stroke. No one suspected the truth—that the source of Mary's agony had come from the very medicine she had trusted to ease her pain.

Mary McFarland was a young mother trying to balance work and raising two children ages one and four. She wouldn't survive the night. Her ordinary headache had become the entry point to something far darker. An invisible hand had guided her to a poisoned bottle, one of many scattered across suburban shelves like silent traps.

LOMBARD TIMELINE

On September 25, 1982, Dan took me to see the 1982 re-release of *Star Wars: Episode IV – A New Hope* at the Yorktown theater. It wasn't yet dark when we arrived. The excitement of the movie was nothing but a smokescreen for what really mattered that night. Before the tickets were purchased, he left me waiting in the car under the dull glow of the parking lot lights. He said he was running inside to grab candy for the movie.

Ten minutes. That was all. But 10 minutes is more than enough time when you already know where you're going. When you already know what you're about to do. He disappeared into the mall. He was swallowed up by its fluorescent corridors. When he returned, he carried nothing more than pockets full of candy and a casual grin, as if nothing had happened.

But something had. Somewhere in that span of minutes, among the Woolworth aisles just steps from where Mary McFarland herself would shop, a bottle was left behind. It sat waiting. It looked innocent in appearance but in truth, it was deadly. He may have even seen her in the mall. The bomb had been placed.

This wasn't chance. It was calculated. A bottle laid like a trap, hidden in plain sight, by a man in a fireman's jacket. Its true purpose was known only to the one who placed it there. Dan would have placed this box at the back of the other boxes.

MARY MCFARLAND'S BOTTLE

Mary McFarland purchased a 50-count bottle of Extra Strength Tylenol from Woolworth in Yorktown Center Mall in Lombard. A container in her purse was later found to contain 10 extra strength capsules, five of which contained cyanide. A search of Mary's residence produced one empty Tylenol bottle and one containing 34 extra strength capsules. One of those capsules contained cyanide.

Poisons offer a quiet alternative to things that go *boom* in the night…

SEPTEMBER 29, 1982 – PAULA PRINCE, CHICAGO, ILLINOIS

Paula Jean Prince was just 35 years old. A flight attendant for United Airlines, she was the only one of the Tylenol victims who lived in the city of Chicago. After a weary journey from Las Vegas to O'Hare, she, like so many others that week, sought relief from a cold. She stopped at Walgreens on her way home on September 29. She purchased what she believed was a simple solution.

Extra Strength Tylenol. The transaction was captured by an ATM's lens, turning everyday medicine into a piece of chilling evidence.

Later that evening, exhaustion and illness overcame her. A bottle rested on her bathroom counter, its cap off. An ordinary tableau, soon to become tragic. Paula never made it to bed. She was found lifeless in her apartment, the quiet of her home forever shattered. She became the seventh and final victim in this deliberate wave of poisoning.

The horror lies not just in her death, but in the terrifying normalcy. Here she was, a woman traveling for work. Returning to her private world. Trusting a medicine deemed safe. She will forever be tied to the story of Mary Kellerman, the Janus family, Mary Reiner, and Mary McFarland by the simplest and most relatable of acts, reaching for pain relief. That is what makes this so unbearable.

CHICAGO TIMELINE

On Saturday, September 11, 1982, Dan took me to the Cubs versus Expos game. What should have been a day of baseball became something else entirely. On the way home, we stopped at a gas station. I had mentioned to him that I had never been to Lincoln Park Zoo. He hadn't forgotten. He never forgot small details because he could twist them into cover.

After filling the tank, he insisted on a walk down LaSalle to the Walgreens on Wells. He bought us each a can of Coke. To me, it felt unnecessary, contrived, a ruse so small it seemed almost unnoticeable. But beneath it was something heavier. He wasn't thirsty, and he wasn't indulging me. He was watching, measuring, marking. What I didn't know then was that we were standing inside his reconnaissance, the opening strokes of a mission he had already begun in his head. He wasn't scoping out soda. He was scoping out where to leave his poison.

Two weeks later, on September 25, we returned to Chicago. This time, the cover story was the zoo, and he brought Justin along. My little brother and I spent 45 long minutes alone at Lincoln Park Zoo while Dan vanished in the direction of Wells Street. He claimed that he needed to cash a check at Dominick's. A flimsy excuse, one that should have raised suspicion. It did with me at the time.

He said he hadn't brought any cash with him. It was easy for him. He carried authority on his shoulders, a red jacket from the Lyons Fire Department that made him untouchable. Who would question a man like that?

I would later learn that both Walgreens and Dominick's on Wells had become crime scenes. Bottles sat there, waiting, placed while I stood unknowingly as his cover. From the zoo, the walk to Wells Avenue was eight blocks. Thirteen minutes at most each way. That left nearly 10 minutes unaccounted for at each location, time enough for him to disappear into the aisles. Time enough to set his traps. Time enough to walk back calm, composed, and smiling, as though nothing had happened.

The truth is that while I waited with Justin at Lincoln Park Zoo, with its cages and enclosures built to contain predators, the most dangerous predator of all was already loose. He had walked into the city with his red jacket and his cold precision. He walked out, leaving behind bottles that would carry death home in ordinary shopping bags. Dan would have placed these boxes at the back of the other boxes.

PAULA PRINCE'S BOTTLE

Paula Prince purchased a 24-count bottle of Extra Strength Tylenol from a Walgreens in Chicago's Old Town neighborhood around 9:16 p.m. on Sept. 29, 1982. A later examination of the bottle revealed that it contained 23 extra strength capsules, four of which contained cyanide. Another tainted bottle of Extra Strength Tylenol was recovered next door at Dominick's.

SECTION FIVE

CHAPTER SEVEN: OCTOBER 1982

For those of you who weren't alive in 1982, or who were alive but too young to remember, let me paint a picture and take you there. I want you to really understand what life looked like, what information felt like, and how utterly different the air we breathed was compared to today.

In 1982, ATM cards weren't common. I know there is a photograph of Paula Prince purchasing her final bottle of Tylenol, and in the foreground are two boys at an ATM. My family didn't have one. I doubt that the Bank of Lyons even issued them at that time. What Dan mentioned that day at the zoo about cashing a check at Dominick's reflected the standard practice for families like mine. If you needed cash, you cashed a check at a store or went through the bank teller and received money that way.

Another thing about 1982: the news didn't chase us down. There was no 24/7 news cycle pulsing through glowing screens. We didn't carry phones in our pockets, feeding us an endless drip of headlines. Social media didn't exist. If you wanted to hear what was happening in the world, you had to go find it yourself. I sometimes joke that the closest thing we had to social media was hanging out at the mall and catching up on gossip. That was our social media in the 1980s. I also joke about just how difficult it was back then to try and text on a rotary phone. I generally just get a blank stare with that one.

Back then, news consumption was a choice. A deliberate act. You could pick up a newspaper. You could buy a magazine. Maybe you would catch a short bulletin breaking into your favorite songs on B-96, Q101, or Oldies 104.3. But if you wanted television news, you had to be sitting in front of your TV at the right time. In Chicago, the news came at set hours: 5:00, 7:00, 9:00, maybe 10:00. That was it. There were no endless channels dissecting every detail. There was no scrolling, no constant streaming, just appointed times and a handful of trusted anchors.

And because of that, there was also no constant, exhausting flood of political warfare. No endless shouting matches of left against right, red against blue. If politics came up, it might be a grunt, an exclamation, a passing remark. And then it was gone. Life moved on. The air was quieter.

So, imagine when the cyanide murders hit in late 1982. The words didn't slam into every household on repeat the way they would today. I can recall hearing about it, maybe on the radio: "Another cyanide-laced bottle of Tylenol has been found in the Chicagoland area." That was it. A sentence. A chilling one. And then silence.

But the silence didn't mean it wasn't real. I remember the fear in the air. People still talked. Kids whispered at school. Adults muttered in the grocery stores. But among my age group, the biggest heartbreak was simple and childish. Halloween was canceled. Just like that, a piece of our childhood was stripped away.

There was no mass coverage, no daily scroll of headlines. We weren't bombarded with updates. Trick-or-treating was called off, and then the conversations faded into hushed tones. If you wanted to know more, you had to dig. And most people didn't.

Even now, as I look back through the media archives of 1982, I find surprisingly little. Especially about the victims. The first week or so after the murders, people were still piecing it all together. It was a tragedy, yes. But it wasn't served up in the relentless, in-your-face way that tragedies are now. The story grew slowly, word of mouth carrying it like an ember drifting through neighborhoods. You heard it if you happened to catch it. You lived it if you were close enough.

Otherwise, it was more shadow than spotlight.

And that is what I need you to understand. In 1982, the horror was real, but the coverage wasn't constant. The fear spread differently. It seeped. It lingered. It whispered.

TUESDAY, OCTOBER 5, 1982

I cannot tell you the exact time, But I can tell you the exact place. Our living room. The burnt-orange carpet under my legs. The 24-inch color TV balanced on a plastic stand designed to look like wood. The archway leading to the hall is just off to the side. I still see it clearly. The window nearby looked out onto Gage Avenue. Dan sat in his chair next to the window, the very spot where his hospice bed would be placed and where he would die decades later almost to the day. The same exact spot where he confessed to this crime that he was hiding.

We didn't watch the news often. That day, however, he demanded it. Channel 7. *ABC News*. Joel Daly's voice, melting through the speakers. I sat cross-legged on the carpet. Silent. Still. My mind was searching for an escape route out of that room. I didn't like being anywhere near him after the day at Busse Woods.

The segment arrived. There were three caskets in a Catholic Church. St. Philomena's Catholic Church, to be exact. The names echoed through the broadcast. Adam. Stanley. Theresa Janus. The church was swollen with grief. Families. Friends. Coworkers. All cloaked in black sorrow. Archbishop Joseph Louis Bernardin sprinkled holy water over the caskets.

"I wish, as your pastor, I could relieve you of your burden of sorrow. But I can't do that, and so I offer you my sympathy, love, and prayers."

His gestures were solemn, his voice steady. The moment carved itself into me. I felt it. My chest ached with it. The weight of other people's suffering pressed through the television and into me. I could feel their pain and sorrow through the airwaves.

For a flicker of time, I believed the silence in the room held the same reverence from Dan. I was wrong.

Dan's breathing shifted. Quick. Shallow. I knew the rhythm. I knew the build. Then his words broke the stillness like a hammer through glass.

"Great. Three fucking. Holy. Catholic Martyrs."

It was six words that landed like blows to the skull. They split the air. They split me. Compassion turned to rage in an instant.

I snapped my head toward him. My eyes locked on his. His smirk burned hotter than the words. "What exactly is that supposed to mean?" My voice was sharp. My voice was shaking. But my voice was mine.

His nostrils flared. Disgust. Anger. Contempt. All at me.

He hated me for standing with the victims. In his mind, I had betrayed him, even though I had no idea at the time.

I pressed harder. "No, seriously. What does that even mean?"

His reply struck like a whip. "None of your fucking business is what that means."

I rose up. My voice rose higher. My rage caught fire. I spat back, unwilling to let it go.

He leaned forward. His eyes were black with fury. His voice was cold. His words were a curse that still festers.

"You think you're so fucking smart? If you're so smart, someday you'll know exactly what it means."

The room spun. My blood boiled. My fists clenched. I stormed out, shaking with fury. Shaking with fear. Shaking with a knowing I couldn't yet name.

That was probably the last TV report I ever saw about the Tylenol murders. Silence after that day. Silence until years later, when the pieces began to fall into placc.

Those six words never left me. They carved a scar so deep it has followed me for over four decades. Not a memory. Not a thought. A wound. His words seared into my mind, my heart, my very marrow.

Because now I understand. He wasn't reacting to the news. He was reacting to himself.

OCTOBER 5, 1982

Originally published October 5, 1982, UPI.

CHICAGO – Archbishop Joseph L. Bernardin embraced grieving relatives at a funeral service for three members of a single family felled by poisoned painkillers.

"I wish as your pastor I could relieve you of your burden of sorrow," the archbishop said during Tuesday's services, "but I can't do that and so I offer you my sympathy, love, and prayers."

Bells tolled as the coffins of Stanley Janus, 25, his wife Theresa, 19, and Stanley's brother, Adam, 27, were taken from separate hearses and carried into St. Hyacinth Church, where 1,000 mourners gathered well before the 10 a.m. mass.

Family members, some sobbing uncontrollably, returned Bernardin's embraces and kissed his ring. The archbishop kissed the caskets before leaving the church in the Polish neighborhood.

A funeral for the seventh victim of cyanide-laced Extra Strength Tylenol, airline flight attendant Paula Prince, 35, was held in her hometown of Omaha, Neb.

Three other poisoning victims were buried during the weekend.

The Januses were among the first victims of the bizarre scheme, which was complicated by official disclosures that Tylenol capsules spiked with strychnine were found in a northern California drugstore.

"It is Jesus who will give you the grace you need to cope with this great loss," said Bernardin, head of the nation's largest Roman Catholic diocese.

A priest sprinkled the caskets with holy water following the service as the choir and congregation sang the hymn "Ave Maria." The Januses were to be buried in adjacent graves at Mary Hill Cemetery in suburban Niles.

Lidia Kochaniuk, a Janus family friend, said the young married couple had just bought a new home and "wanted to start a family."

Dick McAleer, next-door neighbor to Adam Janus, said, "Adam was a good neighbor."

Mourners in Omaha were urged to keep Miss Prince's spirit and enthusiasm alive and pray for understanding of her death.

Jean Regula, 35, a stewardess friend who found Miss Prince's body in her Chicago high-rise apartment last Friday, was among the 350 mourners who attended the hourlong services at Christ the King Roman Catholic Church.

Miss Regula frequently dabbed her eyes and gripped the hand of a companion during the service. She was crying as she left the church.

Tom McGavin, a neighbor and friend in Chicago, described Miss Prince as an "enthusiast over herself and others.

"She charged, strutted and leaped through life with boundless energy... she was always ready for the next event," he said at the eulogy.[5]

---

5. "Chicago—Archbishop Joseph L. Bernardin Embraced Grieving Relatives," UPI, October 5, 1982.

OCTOBER 11, 1982

We were now 11 days into October. Dan hadn't been around much. When he was, he stayed in the lair.

Today was Columbus Day. No school. There was a high of 56 today. This felt more appropriate than the days in the 80s at the end of September and even into October.

The air was definitely heavy. Hyper Dan was gone now. We were pretty much left with Evil Dan. He was always pissed off. Angry. Volatile. This was his normal baseline. The hyper version who made many visits over my summer break and through September was gone.

I didn't miss him. His manic energy was truly exhausting. By the end of September, I was worn out and had gotten a cold. All better now, though.

There were still only small bits of information permeating the air about the Tylenol murders. I heard very little, and what I heard was "... in the Chicagoland area." Chicagoland was a huge area, especially to an 11-year-old. I pictured faraway places, at least far away from Lyons. In those faraway places, people had taken an over-the-counter medication, which, in turn, killed them. My heart broke for the victims. It all seemed so far away. Not once, ever, did I know where the bottles had been purchased or anything about the victims, except what I had seen on the news a few days earlier.

I lived my life with some knowledge of the deaths. To be quite honest, and as it turns out, this is ironic. I had what I now know was a very naïve sense of safety, the thought that my dad was a cop and a firefighter. I felt safe and protected, even though I was quite aware of his demons. I always wanted to think that I was ultimately safe around him.

I was out riding my bike, a blue 10-speed Miyata. I was riding down Fisherman's Terrace, and this overwhelming fear came over me. I had to go home and dump our Tylenol. It was a mission.

Although there wasn't a lot of news floating around, everyone was well aware of the situation.

I turned my bike around. I ended up cutting over to Elm Street. There was an apartment building on the corner of Elm and Highway 66. I used this route when I needed to get back home as quickly as possible. This was one of those times. I cut behind the apartment building through their parking lot.

Fuck. When did they put this speed bump in? I hit the speed bump full force. I'd had a can of Coke in my hand. Not anymore. It was spilled all over a car parked in the lot. I hit the pavement. No helmet, not back in 1982. I really hit the pavement hard. I scratched my powder blue Miyata.

That was okay. I have always been a little uptight about these things. I had touch-up paint in the garage.

I got up. Looked over myself. Good. No broken bones sticking out. A few scrapes. Yes. But no major damage. I checked out my precious Miyata. Scratched, but still operable.

I cautiously finished cutting through the parking lot and cut right over to Gage.

I hung a left. We were three houses in. I hopped off the bike full of purpose. I opened the garage. Put the bike away. Shut the garage door. I entered the house through the garage. That door opens to the stairway that goes down to the basement. To the basement, where my bedroom was located. To the basement, where the lair was located.

I was sure he was down there. I busted in through the kitchen door and ran to the bathroom.

Our medicine cabinet was tall and narrow. Dan had previously installed child-proof latches to the interior of our cabinets to keep Justin out of them after Justin had gotten into the Children's Liquid Tylenol. After Dan had his flashback of his death when he was small from another flavored liquid medicine.

I slightly opened the cabinet door. I reached in and opened the latch. There they were: two new bottles of Extra Strength Tylenol.

I popped them open. No problem. They didn't have childproof lids back then. I pulled out the cotton. I dumped both bottles down the toilet and threw the empty bottles into the garbage can next to the toilet.

Done. I may have just saved my family. I did what many consumers did. Dumped the Tylenol. Case closed.

Then I started thinking, *Why wasn't that Tylenol dumped already?*

NEWSWEEK
OCTOBER 11, 1982, UNITED STATES EDITION
SECTION: NATIONAL AFFAIRS

HEADLINE: THE TYLENOL SCARE

Twelve-year-old Mary Kellerman of Elk Grove Village, Ill., awoke at dawn last Wednesday with a sore throat and a runny nose. Her parents gave her one Extra Strength Tylenol capsule and at 7 a.m. they found her dying on the bathroom floor. Mary Reiner, 27, of nearby Winfield, took two capsules for a mild headache. She was dead within hours at a local hospital. Paramedics found 27-year-old Adam Janus collapsed in his home, his pupils fixed and dilated. Despite emergency room efforts to keep his heart going, Janus died. Later that day his grieving relatives shared a bottle of Extra Strength Tylenol they found in his home. Adam's brother Stanley, 25, died that evening. Theresa, 19, Stanley's wife of three months, held on for two days—until doctors abandoned efforts to save her.

By the weekend seven Chicago-area residents had died and authorities braced for still more victims in what had become the biggest consumer alert in memory and a public-health drama more gripping than any episode of "Quincy." Its source: capsules of Extra Strength Tylenol laced with cyanide, a poison so deadly that it kills within minutes. Tylenol's manufacturer, Johnson & Johnson subsidiary

McNeil Consumer Products Co., recalled two batches of the medication—264,400 bottles nationwide—and the federal Food and Drug Administration warned Americans not to take any Extra Strength Tylenol capsules until the mystery was solved. Drugstores and supermarkets from coast to coast pulled Tylenol products off their shelves. The consumer alert was sadly ironic, given Tylenol's remarkable commercial success as a "safe" aspirin substitute that would not cause stomach upset. In just nine years the acetaminophen-based analgesic had captured 37 percent of the $1.2 billion pain-reliever market, outselling Bayer, Bufferin, Excedrin and Anacin combined.

Investigators in Chicago labeled the deaths homicides, all but ruling out the possibility that the capsules had been contaminated at manufacturing plants. But their theory that individual bottles had been tampered with—perhaps at some point in the distribution chain or, more likely, after they reached retailers—raised the even more chilling prospect that an "over the counter" terrorist was at large, murdering randomly with products millions of Americans used every day. It was a modern version of poisoning the water well, and it struck home with the force of an ancient fear. The routine purchases of everyday life at once seemed ominous and threatening. "I prefer to call this 'American roulette'—Russian roulette with drugs," said Cook County medical examiner Dr. Robert Stein. Panic: Some experts feared that the episode might set off a widespread panic among consumers—and in the wake of the Chicago deaths, there were signs that they could be right. Poison-control centers as far away as San Francisco and New Orleans were flooded with calls from frightened citizens. Some consumers marched into local stores with boxes of Tylenol, demanding their money back—or asking for other painkillers in Tylenol's place. In cities across the country, consumers threw away all the Tylenol on hand, and many discarded other drugs as well. Health officials patiently explained to worried caller after worried caller that if they were able to manage the telephone, they probably did not have cyanide poisoning.

It was by sheer luck—and some diligent medical sleuthing—that investigators zeroed in on the poison pills so quickly. At first, the baffling deaths in separate Chicago suburbs had seemed unrelated. Doctors initially believed that 12-year-old Mary Kellerman, the first victim, died of a stroke; Adam Janus, the second, appeared to have suffered a massive heart attack. But Dr. Thomas Kim at Northwest Community Hospital in Arlington Heights grew suspicious when Janus's brother and sister-in-law were admitted with diluted pupils and very low blood pressure that did not respond to treatment. Kim reported the symptoms to John B. Sullivan Jr., the doctor on duty at the 24-hour Rocky Mountain Poison Center, an advisory agency in Denver. Sullivan asked if the victims could have been exposed to hydrogen sulfide, a poisonous gas. When Kim discounted that possibility, Sullivan replied, "There's only one thing—cyanide." Later, after taking blood samples, Kim called to confirm Sullivan's suspicions. "The levels," he said, "are tremendously high."

"Wild Stab": Almost simultaneously, two off-duty firefighters stumbled upon the Tylenol link. Distraught over her daughter's death, Jeanna Kellerman heard about the mysterious Janus deaths and called Arlington Heights firefighter Philip Cappitelli, the son-in-law of a friend, wondering if he knew any details. Cappitelli called his friend Richard Keyworth, a firefighter in Elk Grove Village. Though Keyworth was on vacation, he had gone into the Elk Grove firehouse to collect his mail, and remembered hearing from paramedics there that Mary Kellerman had taken an Extra Strength Tylenol capsule before collapsing. "This is a wild stab—maybe it's the Tylenol," Keyworth told Cappitelli. Cappitelli then checked with the Arlington

Heights paramedics and learned that the Janus family had taken Extra Strength Tylenol as well.

Within hours, Arlington Heights and Elk Grove Village police had retrieved two bottles from the Janus and Kellerman homes. Both bore the manufacturer's lot number MC2880.

By dawn Thursday the Cook County Medical Examiner's office was at work examining the remaining capsules. "I could smell the cyanide as soon as I opened the containers," said chief toxicologist Michael Shaffer. Ten of the capsules were slightly swollen and discolored, their usual dry white powder replaced with a moist, gray crystalline substance that smelled, characteristically, like bitter almonds. One of the capsules contained as much as 65 milligrams of deadly cyanide—well over the usual lethal dose of 50 milligrams.

Alerted by Chicago authorities early Thursday morning, officials at McNeil and Johnson & Johnson announced an immediate recall of all 93,400 bottles in the MC2880 lot, a batch produced in McNeil's Ft. Washington, Pa., plant and shipped to 31 Eastern and Midwestern states in August. By noon that day, the firm had also dispatched nearly half a million Mailgrams to physicians, hospitals and wholesalers, alerting them to the danger.

But that afternoon the threat widened when authorities linked the sudden death of 31-year-old Mary McFarland of Elmhurst, Ill., to cyanide. Investigators found five contaminated capsules of Extra Strength Tylenol in her purse—and another at her home, in a bottle marked lot 1910MD. Still another bottle, marked lot MC2738, was found—empty—in her trash.

The case of a sixth victim, 27-year-old Mary Reiner of suburban Winfield, who also died Thursday, was even more disturbing. Investigators found four cyanide-laced Extra

Strength Tylenol capsules at her home, but Reiner, who had just delivered her third child, had mixed them with a bottle of Regular Strength Tylenol, and their lot number was untraceable. By Friday McNeil expanded the recall to include all 171,000 bottles of the 1910MD lot, produced at its Round Rock, Texas, plant and shipped to distributors in Chicago and the West. The FDA also urged consumers nationwide not to take Extra Strength Tylenol capsules of any lot number "until the series of deaths in the Chicago area can be clarified."

Officials at McNeil insisted that the poisoning had not occurred at either of its plants, although analytical labs on the premises do keep cyanide supplies on hand. "Our quality control is very rigid," said a Johnson & Johnson spokesman. Most health and law-enforcement authorities agreed. The fact that cyanide-laced capsules had been found in lots produced by both plants and had so far turned up only near Chicago prompted Illinois investigators to conclude that any tampering must have occurred once the shipments reached Illinois. "We have a madman out there," declared Illinois Gov. James Thompson.

Bullhorns: With the worst of the threat seemingly localized there, Chicago health and law enforcement officials took to the streets to warn area residents of the danger, urging them not to take Extra Strength Tylenol capsules and to bring suspect bottles to police for testing and possible evidence. Police cruised neighborhoods, shouting over bullhorns. Boy Scout troops went door to door and church groups launched telephone drives to reach shut-ins or elderly citizens who might not have heard radio and TV warnings.

School officials sent notices home with children, and on some buses and trains, transit workers spread the word. Police made the rounds of taverns far into the night, and anticyanide kits, complete with antidotes, were distributed to all paramedic units.

The warnings apparently never reached at least one Chicago resident. Late Friday night police found the body of a seventh victim, 35-year-old flight attendant Paula Prince, lying in her Near North Side apartment—just steps away from a bottle of Extra Strength Tylenol capsules. The pills were from yet another lot number, 1801MA, and Prince was the first victim found in Chicago, not its suburbs. An autopsy revealed that a suspected eighth victim—an 18-year-old suburban Summit resident who died suddenly Friday and had Extra Strength Tylenol capsules in his locker—was not, in fact, a victim of cyanide poisoning. But some authorities grimly feared that still more bodies -- perhaps those of shut-ins or single people—might be discovered even days after they took contaminated capsules.

There were false alarms elsewhere around the country. A 72-year-old man died in Livingston, Texas, after taking Extra Strength Tylenol; an autopsy revealed he'd had a stroke. A Cleveland- area woman who had taken the capsules was treated for low-level cyanide poisoning, but health officials found no trace of poison in her remaining capsules and they pointed out that minute traces of cyanide can be ingested by eating some types of fish or unwashed fruit.

Still, some poison experts were taking no chances. The Pittsburgh Poison Center sent nine people who complained of nausea and tingling feet to area hospitals. Six were kept overnight for observation. "The early signs of cyanide poisoning can resemble anything from the common cold to hyperventilation," said the center's director, Dr. Richard Moriarty. "We decided to play it conservatively." Other symptoms include sudden headache, nausea, vomiting and extreme agitation. After their onset, death usually occurs swiftly.

"It's like the old spy movies—you crunch down on it, and you're dead," said Dr. James Easton of the Massachusetts Poison Control System. At Georgia's Regional Poison Control Center in Atlanta, Fred Graves became so weary of dispelling fears about minor physical complaints that he began asking callers why they had taken Extra Strength Tylenol in the first place. "Invariably," he said, "the answer came that they were already sick."

Betting: Across the country, citizens received confusing signals from local health authorities about just what threat Tylenol posed. Some state health departments went far beyond the FDA's warning and banned sales of all Tylenol products—including tablets and liquids. Authorities in San Francisco warned consumers not to flush Tylenol down toilets, lest they contaminate the sewer system. Some retail stores, meanwhile, removed only the suspect lots of Extra Strength Tylenol from their shelves while others stopped sales of Tylenol in all forms. And in one curious measure of the public mood, state lottery officials in New Hampshire, Pennsylvania, and Rhode Island had to halt betting on the numbers 2880 and 1910 when wagers reached maximum "liability" levels.

In Chicago, though, the mood was deadly serious. On Saturday officials found poisoned capsules in an unsold bottle of Tylenol they had removed from a store for testing. Investigators from 15 federal, state and local law-enforcement agencies searched for clues to the Tylenol terrorist—or even an apparent method to his madness. Investigators searched police records for suspects who had used poisoned medicines in the past and sought lists of employees at all wholesalers, distributors and retailers who had access to the shipments somewhere along the line. Since two tainted bottles had been purchased at outlets of Jewel warehouse. But other bottles were traced to unrelated stores.

"In Illinois alone, there are 100 distribution points—and 11,000 retail outlets," said chief investigator Tyrone Fahner, Illinois's attorney general.

Reward: Many experts thought it was unlikely that any tampering occurred along the distribution chain, since packages of Tylenol are "shrink-wrapped" in plastic in groups of six at the factory, and adulterating individual bottles before they reached retail stores would be readily apparent from the broken wrapping.

Some investigators had not discounted the notion that the contamination occurred at the McNeil plant or plants—either deliberately or by accident. Late last week McNeil officials, who have offered a $100,000 reward for information leading to a conviction in the case, backed away from initial assertions that no cyanide was used at the firm.

Still, the most likely theory was that someone had simply removed individual bottles from retail stores—selected, perhaps, at random—filled a few capsules with the deadly poison, and sneaked them back onto the shelves for unsuspecting consumers to purchase. If so, the culprit could be virtually anyone—a disgruntled employee, for example, of McNeil or Johnson & Johnson* or an overzealous competitor; after all, aspirin manufacturers, bloodied by Tylenol in the battle for market shares and lately stung by government studies suggesting a link to Reye's syndrome, seemed to have the most to gain from the Tylenol scare. But many experts thought that the culprit was simply a psychopath with a diabolical idea for anonymous murder.

*The damage to Johnson & Johnson could be considerable. Although company stock rebounded last week from a quick 3-point drop after the deaths were made public, the long-term danger was that the good name of a best-selling product would be irreparably damaged. Tylenol is the corporation's biggest single revenue producer; analysts estimate that the poisoning episode could result in losses of $50 million.

If that is the case, investigators face an extraordinary task in tracking down the madman. He could switch products or poisons or locales or lie low for months. For nearly a year, California officials have grappled with a similar product-sabotage case, though it is apparently confined to one supermarket chain, Alpha Beta Food Markets in a small part of Los Angeles. It began last December when eight people were injured using eyedrops found to contain bleach or acid. The stores kept the drops off the shelves for eight months, then sold them restrictively. Then in July, two weeks after regular sales resumed, two more injuries were reported and eight more contaminated bottles found. In August customers reported finding mineral spirits, a type of paint thinner, in one bottle of Skagg's oil and one bottle of laxative. The FBI is investigating—and there are hints that extortion might be involved. But so far, no arrests have been made.

"Consumers really don't have a defense" against such random attacks, says Susan Bond, supervisor for the food and drug division of California's Department of Health Services, who has followed the case closely. FDA deputy commissioner Mark Novitch conceded last week that for all the FDA's tests and standards and requirements, "there is no system we can devise to guarantee that people are protected against a bizarre situation." Some experts, including Bond, have long argued that all over-the-counter medicines should be individually sealed at the factory to guard against undetected tampering, a consumer cause that gained much momentum last week. Chicago Mayor Jane Byrne, for one, proposed a city ordinance that would require all OTC medicines sold there to carry protective seals.

No Guarantee: But if individual medications need protective seals, perhaps so do individual fruits, vegetables and a wide range of other products. Even then, there would be no guarantee of safety, and a madman determined to harm consumers would surely find some way to thwart the precautions. "The magnitude of the possibilities is what frightens me," said Illinois Department of Public Health toxicologist John J. Spikes last week. "We know what we are dealing with. We just don't know when and how." Or, most disturbing of all, why—and whether similar horrors can be prevented in the future.[6]

---

6. Melinda Beck with Sylvester Monroe in Ft. Washington, Mary Hager in Washington, and Ron LaFramboise, "The Tylenol Scare," *Newsweek*, October 11, 1982, United States Edition, National Affairs, 32.

FRIDAY, OCTOBER 15, 1982 – JUSTIN'S FOURTH BIRTHDAY

I was up around 7:30 this morning. The air felt heavy and quiet. It was like the day itself already carried a burden it didn't want to bear. I hadn't seen much of Dan these past two weeks. His absence didn't feel like relief. It was more like the silence of something lurking, waiting to reappear.

Is he back at Electro-Motive? Who knows. Who cares. He slips in and out of routines like a shadow with no anchor. After what he said during the news. After Busse Woods. After the things that have sat festering in the air.

I found myself asking questions I shouldn't have to ask. What kind of man thinks that way? What kind of man talks about death like it's a joke? Was it a puzzle to be solved or a prize to be claimed? These weren't the questions children should be carrying in their heads. But there I was, dragging them with me like chains.

More questions than answers. Always more.

Today should have been simple. It was Justin's birthday. My mom baked him a cake, frosted with the kind of plain sweetness that said she was trying. We sang "Happy Birthday" while Justin stared at the candles like they were the only light in this whole house. For a moment, maybe they were.

The house was subdued and unnaturally quiet, as though even the walls understood that joy here was conditional. It was granted for brief moments and snatched away without warning. The kind of quiet that leaves you wondering if it's safety or just the eye of a storm.

We were planning a birthday party for him on Sunday. Another cake from Weber's. Store-bought, neat, decorated, presentable. A mask in the shape of frosting. I could already see it. When everyone arrived, the house would dress itself up in false cheer. We would all play our parts as if nothing was fractured. As if everything was perfect. And when the last guest left, the masks would drop. The truth would hang in the air again. Thick and suffocating.

This is bullshit.

TYLENOL NOTE SUSPECT HUNTED

Detectives uncover link to 1978 murder in Kansas City
By Ronald Koziol and John O'Brien

A nationwide search for a suspect in a $1 million extortion attempt linked to the Tylenol-cyanide killings was intensified Thursday as authorities linked the suspect to a 1978 murder in Kansas City, Mo.

At a press conference Thursday, Atty. Gen. Tyrone Fahner, coordinator of a multi-agency task force investigating the deaths of seven persons from cyanide-laced Extra Strength Tylenol capsules, said the suspect and his wife were wanted on charges arising from the extortion note and for questioning in the Tylenol murders.

"We want the couple back here to pursue the Tylenol murders," Fahner said. But he acknowledged that, at the present time, "we have no direct evidence that those two people are responsible for the Tylenol cyanide deaths."

Investigators confirmed that Robert Richardson, who has been identified as the alleged writer of a letter demanding $1 million from Johnson & Johnson, parent firm of the Tylenol manufacturer, was in fact James W. Lewis. Lewis was charged with the kidnapping and dismemberment of an adult in Kansas City in 1978.

In that case, police found the mummified body of the victim, Raymond West, 72, in an attic in August 1978. His death had been caused by multiple skull fractures, and his legs had been severed.

The case against Lewis was dismissed by a Missouri judge who ruled that his arrest and the seizure of his property was illegal.

But authorities said the seized property, which was not returned to Lewis, included textbooks and journals which described the use of various poisons and their effects on human beings.

The breakthrough in the extortion case came when three homicide detectives from Kansas City arrived in Chicago to consult with Tylenol task force investigators. They brought with them evidence that tied Richardson positively to Lewis.

The disclosures about Lewis surfaced a day after a 48-year-old dockhand at a Jewel Food warehouse in Melrose Park was released on bond after it was determined that a substance in his apartment was not cyanide, as suspected, but a nontoxic cleansing agent.

The dockhand, Roger R. Arnold, 48, had been charged with aggravated assault and four weapons violations, all misdemeanors, and Police Supt. Richard Brzeczek said Thursday that Arnold was not considered a suspect in the Tylenol deaths.

But Brzeczek said Arnold was not completely out of the picture either. "There is not enough to charge or eliminate Arnold," Brzeczek said.

It is believed that Lewis assumed the Richardson identity after his wife came into possession of a wallet belonging to a man of that name. The extortion note to Johnson & Johnson demanded that $1 million be placed into an account at a large Chicago bank "if you want to stop the killing." It then warned the company not to "involve the FBI or local Chicago authorities… A couple of phone calls by me will undo anything you can possibly do."

Lewis also is known to have been sought for some time on another federal complaint charging him with unlawful flight to avoid prosecution in Kansas City on a theft charge.

The FBI has obtained warrants for Lewis on an extortion charge and for his wife on a charge of using a fictitious Social Security number in seeking employment in Chicago, according to a spokesman for Edward D. Hegarty, Chicago FBI chief.

Lewis' two identities were brought to light when Kansas City residents and police identified a photo of "Richardson" in the Kansas City Times as that of Lewis, investigators said. The photo, widely disseminated by the FBI because of the extortion warrant issued for Richardson, was supplied to the authorities by The Tribune, which last July 26 ran an essay by "Richardson" entitled A Slice of Chicago Life.

Lewis was a tax accountant in Kansas City at the time of the slayings. While Lewis was in Chicago, he was employed as an accountant in a private tax service on Broadway. Kansas City police connected Lewis with the slaying of West when Lewis attempted to cash a check using West's name after the victim had been reported missing.

"An intensive search for the couple is underway here and in Kansas City," according to Thomas E. Hadway, assistant special agent in charge of the Chicago FBI office.

Authorities said Lewis was in Chicago for about nine months, until he and his wife abruptly left their second-floor apartment on Belden Avenue on Sept. 3, leaving an Amarillo, Texas, forwarding address that proved false.

Lewis, 36, is a native of rural Jasper County, Mo., 150 miles south of Kansas City. Investigators identified his wife, who in Chicago used the name Nancy Richardson, as Leann Miller Lewis, now 35 years old.

As Nancy Richardson, Mrs. Lewis worked for a now-defunct Chicago travel agency operated by a North Shore businessman whose inactive bank account number figured in the $1 million extortion letter linked to "Richardson."

Mrs. Lewis was one of four former employees named by the businessman as possibly disgruntled workers who might want to embarrass him. The other three were interviewed by authorities.

Authorities said the four had complained that their final paychecks, issued when the travel firm closed in April, bounced.

A photograph of "Mrs. Richardson" or Mrs. Lewis was circulated by authorities, who obtained it from a bank where she worked in Chicago. The identification of the Lewis couple is "an important lead, since Lewis was involved in a murder before," Fahner said. "Yes, this has great significance."

Lewis was described as 6 feet 1 inch tall, weighing about 170 pounds, with brown hair. He wears wire-rimmed glasses and has been known to wear a full beard. His wife was described as dark- haired and heavyset.

It is also known that Lewis has described himself as a freelance computer consultant.

Arnold, meanwhile, was free on $6,000 bond. After his release, Arnold said his arrest had been "blown way out of proportion."

"I had nothing to do with this Tylenol thing at all. They can think what they want," he said.

After his arrest, Arnold consented to a police search of his home, where officers found four pistols and a carbine. He was then charged with five misdemeanor counts of failure to register a weapon.

During the search of his home, police also found a handbook describing various ways to kill persons which included a chapter on how to poison people with cyanide-filled capsules.

"Based on what we know about Mr. Arnold, it does not appear likely that he is the main suspect in this case," said a spokesman for Fahner's office.[7]

7. Ronald Koziol and John O'Brien, "Tylenol Note Suspect Hunted: Detectives Uncover Link to 1978 Murder in Kansas City," *Chicago Tribune*, October 15, 1982.

SATURDAY, OCTOBER 16, 1982 – A LITTLE HOUSE CLEANING

Justin's cake from Weber's Bakery was waiting, set aside for us to pick up first thing in the morning. Tomorrow we were supposed to have people over. That always made things bearable. At the very least, when other people were around, the air didn't feel so heavy.

But lately, the weight in the house had thickened. Dan's energy was sharper, unpredictable, and just beneath the surface. Manic.

The manhunt was everywhere. The Tylenol killer was loose, and the city pulsed with rumor. Headlines screamed from *Tribune* racks, while glossy *Newsweek* covers stared from store shelves. Yet inside our house, we were strangely insulated. The news still only slipped through in fragments. Snatched from a flash on the television, a stray line on the radio, a headline glimpsed and quickly folded away. The real story lived outside, beyond our walls.

Upstairs, my mother worked through her ritual of pre-company cleaning. Floors scrubbed. Counters wiped down. Dusting. Bathroom bleached to perfection. The house always appeared immaculate. I never understood how she managed it. She carried schoolwork on her shoulders. She took care of us. She carried bruises on her body. She carried Dan's rage like a shadow. He refused to let her study until every child had gone to bed. His fists and his words followed her into the dark. His insecurity demanded it.

One night, he cornered her in the bathroom.

"You like those pearly whites of yours? You think that by becoming a nurse with your fancy degree, you'll leave me for some doctor? I'll knock those pretty white teeth down your fucking throat."

That was our life on Gage Avenue in 1982.

The violence never paused. It only shifted its mask. My mother tried to hold the house together. She tried to give Justin and Liz something that resembled normal. They were too young to see the cracks. Too young to know the weight of memory. I wasn't too young. Every word was burned into me.

So, she cleaned upstairs, preparing for company.

Dan prowled below, in the lair. His movements precise. His actions deliberate. He was doing a bit of cleaning as well. In the lair. At 11 years old, I sensed the wrongness. Today, as a man of law, I have the words: destruction of evidence. He wasn't cleaning. He was erasing.

My mother asked me to straighten my room. I didn't protest. I never gave her grief. She carried enough. I saw it in her eyes, a hardness that never left. A plea unspoken.

So, down the stairs I went. I avoided the squeaky step halfway down.

As I reached the bottom of the stairs, there he was. In the lair. Lights, camera, action.

Here we go. I stepped off the last stair. The lair waited. Dim light. The stink of oil and dust. Silence broken only by Dan's movements.

A yellow Shell Oil drum stood between us. There was always one there. It was always shifting places. It was always filled with something. Electro-Motive property, stolen and dragged into our basement. Sometimes it disappeared. Sometimes another appeared. Always replaced. Always a secret. I have to wonder where all of those barrels disappeared to.

Today, this barrel held his fury. Dan moved fast, manic, tossing objects inside. His eyes were wild, his hands shaking. He didn't see me at first. I walked closer, plain as day. He stayed consumed by his frenzy.

Then he noticed. His body snapped toward me. He hurled something into the drum. A glint of gold. My eyes caught it. I reached in and pulled out a ring.

A Masonic ring. Heavy gold. Black onyx inlay. A bold letter "G." Compass and square. A diamond set deep. Too large for a child's hand. Too wrong for an 11-year-old to hold.

Dan ripped it from my fingers. His voice exploded. "What the fuck is wrong with you? Don't get your fingerprints on that."

He shoved it back into the barrel, his focus locked on the contents again. He muttered. He shifted. He dug deeper.

I leaned forward, my heart slamming against my ribs. I dared a second look. Inside, terror stacked itself like layers of rot.

I did it. I looked with intent.

The black-and-white *Anarchist Cookbook*. The Masonic ring glinted under scraps.

The pink midget cup. Empty. Lid gone. Stacks of *Poor Man's James Bond*.

The thing that looked like a rotary phone dial from American Science & Surplus. More papers. Typed. All marked with a title: *How to Kill*.

Newspaper clipping. Lots of them.

Beneath them, the green strap of a Timex watch. Khaki. The same watch I had found near First Avenue. The portion of the strap that I saw was screaming, "Look at me!" The rest of it was buried under the papers.

The air in the lair thickened. I couldn't breathe. My 11-year-old eyes saw everything. My 11-year-old mind understood nothing. My adult mind sees it now. Every piece was evidence. Every item was a message. Every object was representative of death.

I went to my room. I straightened it. Hours later, the sound came—Dan dragging the barrel across the basement floor. The groan of steel against cement. The thud at the door. A step from the laundry room to the outside.

SCREEEEEEEEEEECH.

The sound tore through the house. The bottom of the barrel scraped, clawing at the stairs. Each drag another shriek. Each movement, a scream of metal against wood. He hauled it out into the yard.

What was he doing now?

I waited. Minutes stretched like hours. Silence returned. I crept up, avoiding the creaky stair halfway up. I reached the kitchen window.

There he stood. With the barrel. On the concrete in front of our outdoor fireplace.

He carried the round, red gas can. The metal one for the lawnmower. He poured. He doused. He baptized the barrel in gasoline.

Then fire. A bloom of orange. A roar of heat. He loved fire. He loved explosions.

The barrel became a furnace. Flames clawed skyward. Sparks spat into the night. Evidence was reduced to smoke. Secrets turned into ash. He stood over it like a priest. A private ritual. A one-man bonfire. A celebration of destruction.

When it ended, nothing would remain. No trace. No proof. Only silence.

This column was originally published in the Chicago Tribune *on October 16, 1982.*

TYRONE AND TYLENOL

CHICAGO—[Political journalist] David Axelrod wrote an article implying Atty. Gen. Tyrone Fahner is gaining political strength from the Tylenol tragedy.

I don't know if Fahner is gaining, but he has helped the perpetrator by publicly labeling him a madman on television. Although this may respond to the emotionalism of the tragedy, it does not respond to the weight of the situation. If the person is ever caught, his defense has been aided admirably by Fahner's statements.

I believe the accused person certainly would use the insanity defense, and who better to back up his claim than the man responsible for his prosecution, Fahner.

In this era of backlash from insanity defense, like that of John Hinckley, Fahner would be well advised to do and not talk. It would be a real crime if the perpetrator were able to "beat the rap" through an insanity plea, a plea Fahner's irresponsibility could help the Tylenol poisoner obtain.

Vince M. Lizzo[8]

That was it for this day. Yes, there were some reprints of previous stories. But this was it. The story started with the victims. Jumped to how much damage Johnson & Johnson

---

8. David Axelrod, "Tyrone and Tylenol," *Chicago Tribune*, October 16, 1982.

would have to overcome. Focused in on John Lewis. And now the story was turning political.

Things were different in 1982.

SUNDAY, OCTOBER 17, 1982 – THE OPEN (LAIR) HOUSE

We didn't go to church this morning. It was so much work getting ready for a four-year-old's birthday party.

The house was spotlessly clean. We were all dressed and ready for action.

We're all in our places with bright shiny faces.

I did walk down to Sam's earlier this afternoon with my dollar in hand and picked up the Sunday *Chicago Tribune*.

I walked it back and set it in a rack that sat next to Dan's chair near the window.

At about 4:00, people started arriving. I did notice that, for some reason, this birthday party was much more labor-intensive than our previous soiree for Liz and me last July.

Oh well. We were most definitely showing up and showing out. I was upstairs pretty much all day today. It was calm. It was nice. As usual, though, something felt off.

I ran down to my room at about 4:15, and I saw the strangest thing.

The lair door stood open. Yes. Fully open. The lair stood exposed. The door was wide open, lights blazing. The fluorescents were buzzing like a swarm.

BUZZZZZZZ.

That relentless hum drilled into my skull.

He had scrubbed it clean. The floor gleamed. No clutter. No dust. Not a trace of yesterday's chaos. Every tool was lined up in order. Locksmith equipment sharp, glinting. His gray magnifying lamp was burning hot, magnifying shadows across steel. The air felt staged, unnatural, like a set built for a performance no one had asked to attend.

The plastic shades were up. Orange blinds, once sealed tight, now surrendered. Sunlight pierced the room where no light ever lived. It made the space feel wrong. Too open. Too bright. An open secret screaming to be noticed.

Gone were the midget cups. Gone were the books, *The Anarchist Cookbook, Poor Man's James Bond, How to Kill.* The evidence had been erased, replaced with spotless silence.

I told myself it was theater. He wanted it to look normal. He wanted me to believe it had always been this way. He wanted me to forget.

But it was new. Too new. Shelves had appeared where none had stood before. Small, cheap rectangles, stacked like relics from an old hotel lobby. They covered the wall/door. They swallowed the seams I had bloodied my hands on.

It was a disguise. It was preparation hiding in plain sight. Exactly like stalking your prey. I turned around and was walking out of the lair door.

And there he was. Now he was Smilin' Dan. He had a smirk on his face that went from ear to ear. That smirk was plastered there. Not moving. It looked as if he'd had the smirk attached permanently by a plastic surgeon.

"What do you think about the workshop?" He was taunting me.

"Looks good. First time I've ever seen it clean," I replied.

He was staring me down now. I stared back.

"Well, I'm off to the party now," I said, and upstairs I went.

That fucker! I was thinking.

The way he was taunting me and staring me down. Almost daring me. Daring me for what?

By the end of the night, he had taken pretty much everyone down there to give them the tour of the lair.

Who would suspect a thing? I would. That is who.

This column was originally published in the Chicago Tribune *on October 17, 1982.*

TYLENOL SUSPECT VOLATILE, PROBERS SAY
RONALD KOZIOL AND JOHN O'BRIEN

The man wanted on an extortion charge stemming from the cyanide-spiked Extra Strength Tylenol case was fired from a Chicago accounting job in March when he refused to admit an error in his computation of an income tax statement and became "violent," the suspect's former employer said Saturday.

Investigators searching for James W. Lewis, 36, charged with sending an extortion letter to the parent company of the firm that manufactures Tylenol, were concentrating their efforts in Missouri and Texas, where Lewis and his wife, Leann, 35, were known to have lived and have friends.

But law enforcement officials were not discounting the possibility that the two have fled the country, possibly traveling as far as India.

In Chicago, Ed Leavitt, owner of Ed Leavitt Tax Service, 3327 N. Broadway, told The Tribune that he spent 2½ hours on March 5 correcting a mistake made on a tax return prepared by Lewis, who then was using the pseudonym, Robert Richardson. Lewis had been hired Jan. 20.

When confronted with the error, Lewis became enraged and refused to accept responsibility for it, Leavitt said.

"When I saw how violent he was becoming, I suggested that it would be better off for all of us if he left," Leavitt said. "And he did."

Leavitt said FBI agents told him Lewis was known to get violent with those who fired him.

Leavitt, who has owned the tax service since 1959, said Lewis' résumé had the best qualifications of anyone who ever came to work for him.

That same application was given to the FBI and was analyzed by handwriting experts who allege it was written by the same person who sent an extortion note to Johnson & Johnson, parent company of the firm that manufactures Extra Strength Tylenol, threatening more poisonings if a $1 million demand were not met.

References on Lewis' résumé included dead people, investigators said.

New descriptions of Lewis that Leavitt gave law officials include the fact that he had bad eyes that were always watering, requiring the suspect to constantly swab at his eyes with tissue.

Leavitt also said Lewis asked that his paychecks—usually amounting to about $350 for each 4-day work week—be made out to his wife, identified as "Nancy," because she had an account with a currency exchange across the street.

But Leavitt said he learned Friday from the currency exchange operator that Mrs. Lewis told exchange employees it was she who worked for Leavitt's company.

The couple operated an accounting firm, Lewis & Lewis, in Kansas City, Mo., until last December when, facing fraud charges, they fled, reportedly driving a 1969 Rambler.

Leavitt said he never saw Lewis driving a car during his employment in Chicago.

Lewis was "very competent most of the time, but had a tendency to talk a lot to the clients" and seemed to be a dreamer, Leavitt said.[9]

Once again, all of the focus was on James Lewis. What he did wasn't very smart, but with all of the efforts focused squarely on him, there had been no room to look toward anyone else.

Dan had too much of a sense of safety at this point. Untouchable.

SUNDAY, OCTOBER 31, 1982 – HALLOWEEN

Yes. All festivities had been canceled. The air itself carried unease. Parents whispered warnings at the edges of driveways. Their voices were low and clipped, as if the night might be listening. Razor blades in apples. Poison in candy. The word "Tylenol" was hissed like a curse passed from one porch to another. Halloween had been stolen from us that year, ripped out of the calendar and buried in fear.

Still, small pockets of resistance survived. Our neighborhood party glowed faintly like a lantern in a fog. Mr. and Mrs. Baker opened their home on Fisherman's Terrace. Inside their windows shone amber light against the early dark. The smell of cinnamon and caramel drifted into the street, a promise that not everything had been lost to terror.

---

9. Ronald Koziol and John O'Brien, "Tylenol Suspect Volatile, Probers Say," *Chicago Tribune*, October 17, 1982.

We dressed up anyway. Liz, Justin, and I. Our costumes rustled like paper wings as Mom led us down to the Bakers' house. Her hand was warm, steady, though I knew she wouldn't linger long.

The Bakers' living room pulsed with life. Laughter cracked the heavy silence that had settled over Lyons. Children's voices rose, high-pitched and bright. Breaking like glass against the fear outside. Paper decorations clung to the walls. Pumpkins with crooked smiles, black cats with eyes too wide. Mrs. Baker handed out homemade trick-or-treat bags and pressed still-warm, freshly made caramel apples into small hands. The sweet, sticky smell wrapped around us, defiant in its innocence.

Games erupted. Pin the Tail on the Donkey. The donkey's grin looked sly beneath the pinholes. Twister mats unrolled across hardwood floors, squeaking under small socks and Halloween costumes. I can still hear the thud of children collapsing in tangled heaps, laughter bouncing off the walls, the squeals echoing through the house. For a moment, the world outside of razor blades, poison, and Dan melted away.

It was fun. I remember freezing in place, the noise spinning around me, thinking. This was only two blocks away. Two blocks from the house, where Dan's shadow lay heavy over everything. Two blocks from the place where we lived with hell itself. How could there be such a difference in so little distance?

I felt like I had stepped into another orbit, far away from the orbit of a black hole. A parallel world where light still survived. If I could drift only two blocks and feel joy, maybe someday I could drift farther. Miles, states, oceans away from Dan's gravity. *Stay the course*, I told myself. *Someday, I'll be free of his pull.*

Lost in thought, I glanced at Liz and Justin. Their costumes hung a little loose, their laughter rang too high, still more children than anything else. Their faces were flushed pink from games, their eyes alight with sugar and thrill. They were so small. For one shimmering moment, I let myself imagine a future where we all survived this, where there was a light at the end of the tunnel. It was sunlight, not an oncoming train.

But dreams never lasted long. The laughter began to blur. The air grew heavy again, as though a door had opened and let the cold back in. The sweetness of caramel turned sour in my mouth.

Reality had a way of stepping in, uninvited. Guess who showed up.

Dan showed up.

He was draped in a Halloween costume that only his fractured mind could dream up. His Lyons Police Department uniform hung on him. Every piece of gear was strapped in place. A Maglite on his belt. Handcuffs that clinked with each step. Service weapon gleaming in the low light. His shirt was unbuttoned, spread wide. He was wearing his Superman T-shirt beneath it like some twisted joke.

On his head, a vinyl pig mask. Glossy. Shiny in the Bakers' living room light. The snout caught the glow and made his face into something animal, something obscene.

He slipped through the back door without a sound, moving like a predator, exactly how he had trained me to move. The air shifted before he appeared, the way it does when a storm front pushes through. Arms stretched wide, he lurched into the living room. The sound he made, that low, guttural, half-roar, half-snort like a wild boar rattled the walls.

The room fractured. Children screamed. Shrieks cut through the aroma of caramel and popcorn. Feet slapped against hardwood as they bolted to corners, pressed themselves into walls, scrambled for hiding places. Liz froze, her eyes wide, mouth open. Her voice caught in her throat. Justin turned to stone. He had done this before, the day Dan pressed a loaded gun against his head. He knew that immobility was safer than reaction.

I sat, burning with shame. Burning with rage. Embarrassment flooded my skin, but underneath it churned a hatred so deep it made my chest shake.

Still too young to understand the danger, Liz squealed out, "Super Pig." Her voice was innocent, a tiny bell in a room filled with terror.

Mr. and Mrs. Baker scrambled. Their hands gathered children from corners. They pulled them into the open and corralled the chaos. Faces pale, eyes wide. The air was heavy with sweat, sugar, and fear.

Dan quickly pulled the mask off. His smirk was visible beneath the fluorescent lights. "Don't be scared," he said, voice calm, almost friendly. "It's just me, Mr. Drozd. Your neighborhood beat cop. Here to wish everyone a happy Halloween."

His words dripped with mockery. A wolf dressed in sheep's clothing.

The children crept back, step by step. Lured by the reassurance, they wanted to believe. Their sobs softened. Their screams faded. A fragile calm returned, though the air still crackled with unease.

Dan turned to me. His eyes locked with mine. That look. The look I knew too well. The message was silent, but deafening.

Look what I can do. Look what I can get away with.

The smell of vinyl still lingered in the air. The sound of his boots was heavy on the floor. The sight of his grin burned into my memory. Halloween, stolen. Innocence, shattered. Fear, permanent.

This column was originally published in the Chicago Tribune *on October 31, 1982.*

IN A HANDWRITTEN note to The Chicago Tribune, the man sought nationwide as an extortion suspect in the Tylenol poisoning deaths claims neither he nor his wife was responsible for the seven cyanide murders.

The note was part of an inch-thick packet of material mailed to The Tribune from New York in a manila envelope postmarked Oct. 27. All the papers were turned over to the FBI, which said it had no reason to doubt the material was authentic and sent by James Lewis. The FBI said it could not be absolutely certain until the letters were verified by handwriting analysis.

"As you have probably guessed, my wife and I have not committed the Chicago area Tylenol murders. We do not go around killing people. We never have and we never shall," he wrote in one of the notes to The Tribune, composed with a black, felt-tip pen on white typing paper.

"Contrary to reports we are not armed, unless one means in the anatomical paraplegic sense. We shall never carry weapons no matter how bizarre the police and FBI reports. Domestically, weapons are for two quite similar types of mentalities: [1] criminals & [2] police. We are neither."

The envelope, stamped "first class," arrived in the newspaper's regular Friday morning mail. It was addressed to the City Editor and bore a New York City postmark and $1.53 in postage.

Lewis and his wife, LeAnn, who used the names Robert and Nancy Richardson in Chicago, were last seen in New York Oct. 16 when they checked out of a seedy midtown hotel where they had lived for six weeks. Authorities had said they believed the couple were still in New York but the postmarked envelope to The Tribune was the first indication they remained there or, at least returned there last Wednesday to mail the package.

The FBI and New York City police mobilized a 100-officer search force to renew their hunt for the Lewises after The Tribune turned over the packet.

Law enforcement officials said there were indications the couple had left the city, but since the letter was postmarked in New York, officials have renewed hopes that they are still in the city or nearby.

In the material sent to The Tribune, Lewis signed himself Robert Richardson or R.R. throughout.

Illinois Atty. Gen. Tyrone Fahner, who is heading the task force investigating the case, said Saturday that Lewis should turn himself in. "If you're innocent—as you claim," Fahner said, addressing Lewis, "we'll help you prove your innocence."

The attorney general refused to say whether he believes Lewis is responsible for the murders. "It's as likely as it is not," he said.

The couple became the object of a nationwide search when Chicago authorities connected Lewis with an extortion letter sent to Johnson & Johnson, parent firm of the makers of Tylenol, demanding $1 million "to stop the killings." Kansas City authorities then recognized him as a fugitive wanted there for one count of theft in a land fraud swindle involving an elderly couple.

Most of the material contained in the packet mailed to The Tribune consisted of bank records, court documents and other papers relating to LeAnn Lewis' employment at Lakeside Travel, a defunct Chicago travel agency from which she was fired last March.

At no point did Lewis directly refer to the extortion letter sent to Johnson & Johnson. Police say the letter was in his handwriting.

In one of the notes mailed to The Tribune, Lewis wrote, "I too am a victim, but so what. My situation is not so sad as that of the bereved [sic] families and the memories of their loved ones. I hope the law finds whoever poisoned [sic] those capsules and I would demand capital punishment."

At one point, Lewis claimed he had only tried to do his civic duty by drawing the attention of the law enforcement agencies to his wife's former employer. Lewis charged was involved in illegal moneymaking schemes. It was not clear if this could be a reference to the extortion letter, which demanded that Johnson and Johnson place $1 million in a Chicago bank account belonging to the travel agency owner.

Authorities said the letter may have been part of a vendetta by Lewis against the North Shore businessman who owned the agency. The businessman, who was questioned by police, had identified LeAnn Lewis as a former disgruntled employee who might want to embarrass him after he had fired her for allegedly cashing in phony airline tickets and converting her own share into $300 worth of travel stationery. Subsequently, she complained that her final paycheck had bounced.

As a result of his efforts to bring the businessman's dealings to public attention, Lewis complained, "What a disgusting and callous disrespect for law and order and credibility. Well, all I can say is that this is a very, very sad and sordid affair. Never become an informant. Never try to be a good citizen unless you are prepared for the same treatment by the police and FBI."

Also included in the packet was an elaborate, Rube Goldberg-like cartoon drawn by Lewis and signed "R. Richardson 82" purporting to show the inner workings of Lakeside Travel. In an accompanying note, he added, "This cartoon was drawn in July of this year, but it is still hot, so likely The Trib may print this if you wish. There is no charge."

As verification of his identity, Lewis enclosed a copy of a "Point of View" column he wrote for The Tribune last July on a freelance basis and included the corporate account number on the $50 check paid him.

The column was a brief accounting of what he observed while standing for 10 minutes at State and Madison on a summer afternoon.

As is standard practice, Lewis came to The Tribune with the photograph taken to run with the column. It was this photo, provided by The Tribune to the FBI, that was distributed nationwide and subsequently recognized by law officials in Kansas City.

They identified the bespectacled accountant as a fugitive wanted there for land fraud and also credit card swindles, although there are no formal charges against him for the latter.

Lewis had been charged with murder there in 1978, but the charges had been dropped after a judge ruled Lewis' arrest and seizure of his property was illegal. Kansas City police said earlier this month they were considering reopening the murder investigation.

After a search of their home by Kansas City postal inspectors last December, the Lewises fled to Chicago, where as Robert and Nancy Richardson they operated a grimy two-room apartment at 549 W. Belden Ave. LeAnn, using a false social security number, first got a job at Lakeside Travel but was fired in March, shortly before they relocated.

Lewis, who operated his own tax accountant firm in Kansas City, worked at Ed Leavitt Tax Service, 3327 N. Broadway, for about three months until he, also, was fired after arguing with his employer.

Mrs. Lewis subsequently got another bookkeeping job, this time with a Loop firm. Lewis stayed home at the Belden rooming house, whiling away his hours training the building manager's dog and expounding on his various economic theories.

The couple left Chicago for New York in early September and according to authorities were believed to be there when the poisoning deaths began in the Chicago area four weeks ago.[10]

This was it for Halloween 1982. No search other than harassing the Lewises. No warnings about trick-or-treating. Nothing about the victims or the crime itself. The investigation had turned to James Lewis for the extortion letter.

---

10. "In a Handwritten Note to The Chicago Tribune, the Man Sought Nationwide as an Extortion Suspect in the Tylenol Poisoning Deaths Claims Neither He nor His Wife Was Responsible," *Chicago Tribune*, October 31, 1982.

NOVEMBER 1982
SATURDAY, NOVEMBER 13, 1982

I should have killed you when I had the chance...

It was bitterly cold, the kind of cold that rips the oxygen out of your lungs. Yesterday had reached 60 degrees. Today sank to 29 degrees. The house groaned against the temperature drop. Frost lined the edges of the windows. My skin prickled, but not just from the chill.

Dan's moods shifted like the weather. Violent. Unpredictable. Dangerous.

The plan was simple today. A movie with friends. *Creepshow*. Stephen King. Horror on the screen, but controlled. Predictable. Safer than the horror I lived with daily. My mother agreed to take us. Relief filled me. For one brief moment, I believed the cold outside might be the worst part of this day.

Then Dan entered the kitchen. He carried the storm with him.

"I can drive you guys to the movies. I want to see that movie too," he said.

His voice sounded casual. My gut tightened. I had flashbacks to Busse Woods. His chaos. His threat. My friends would never understand. I wanted no part of it again.

"Oh. I was just planning on going with my friends today," I replied.

The air grew sharper. The walls seemed to lean in. His eyes cut through me like shards of ice. "No. Really. It's no problem. I would love to hang out with you and your friends," he pressed.

I shook my head. I wasn't giving in. "No. I really just wanted Mom to drop us off at the movies so I could hang out with my friends."

That was it. The final spark. Dan flipped.

He shoved me against the wall. The impact, like the temperature outside, stole the breath from my lungs. The wooden chair rail on the kitchen wall bit into my back.

"You little bastard. Who the fuck do you think you are?" His face glowed crimson. Veins bulged. His spit hit my cheek, hot against the icy air of the room.

My body refused to fold. I didn't break. I didn't fall. I didn't crack. My voice rose, louder than the storm outside. I was giving him his Cheshire-Cat-like smirk right back to him. I locked eyes with him.

"You know who I am? I am anybody. But. You."

His nostrils flared. His eyes widened, unblinking. Madness lived there.

He jabbed his finger a few inches from my face. **"I should have killed you when I had the chance."**

The words froze me harder than the temperature outside. No movie monster had ever spoken more truth. I saw it clearly right then and there. He was insane. Utterly broken. Beyond saving.

He turned. Walked away. Left the room colder than before.

I didn't let him win. I wouldn't. I went to the movies with my friends. As planned.

Here we were. Not even two months after the murders. Not a peep today in the newspapers about them.

And there it was. *I should have killed you when I had the chance.*

THURSDAY, NOVEMBER 25, 1982 – THANKSGIVING

This family had been shattered. Not like the families of the victims. Different. But still shattered. Dan was absent. I neither saw him nor cared.

The plan was set. I would spend Thanksgiving at Vic and Jeannie's, Grannie's brother and sister-in-law. Grannie picked us up. Justin. Liz. Me.

The day etched itself into my memory. Forever.

I wore a cream wool sweater. Cable knit. A red shirt beneath. The high reached 37 degrees. The air cut sharply. The cold pressed into every seam of my clothes. Details like that never leave me.

Vic and Jeannie's house stood solid. A Cicero brick bungalow. Warmth radiated from within.

Crossing the threshold, the scent engulfed me. Turkey roasting. Pine incense smoldering. Love layered through it all. My chest filled with it.

The marble floor gleamed under the entry light. A gilded mirror glowed on the wall. Gold candleholders caught the flame. A marble shelf shone beneath, anchored with brackets that gleamed like treasure.

The "fronchroom" stretched before me. That means front room/living room in the proper Chicago vernacular. White carpet spread wall to wall. Plastic runners guarded the path. Feet didn't stray from them.

French Provincial furniture stood proud. The pure white fabric was embroidered with gold. The edges trimmed with shine. Slipcovers of clear plastic kept every thread preserved. A marble coffee table gleamed, its gilded legs strong. Golden velvet drapes framed the bay window. Sheer white curtains softened the light that filtered through.

The bay window cradled its centerpiece—a Venus de Milo swag lamp. Oil dripped endlessly, sliding down thin, clear rods. Rain inside a lamp. A storm captured and tamed.

The room glowed with thought. With intention. With care. Every inch spoke of devotion.

Vic and Jeannie's home was more than brick and plaster. It was a sanctuary. It was a memory. It was love.

This is where this story must rest. For now. This moment carried light. The table glowed with Thanksgiving. I sat still. Surrounded. My parents were absent. Their absence was louder than any words. Yet I remained. Present. Breathing. Watching. The rest of 1982 was a whiter shade of pale.

That was the day I understood. My childhood had ended. I was the adult in my family. The shield. The witness. The survivor. I felt it like a stone inside my chest. Heavy. Permanent. Irrevocable.

That was the day I knew that I alone would have to walk through the madness. I would have to step through the chaos and gather the fragments. It was up to me to piece together what never wanted to be seen. To name what my father had done. To name the demon.

The house smelled of turkey. The voices hummed softly. Love brushed across the table like a warm hand. Still, beneath it all, I could hear the echo. The echo of him. The echo of what he had carved into our souls.

Later, as I searched and sifted for truth, I uncovered more. Too much more. Crimes that bore his mark. Dark stains pressed into places where no one thought to look. I cannot speak of them yet. They will each have their time. Each one demands its own telling. Each one deserves its own reckoning. And yet there is more. Much more. Always more questions than answers.

This moment was the end of innocence. This moment was the beginning of truth.

INFINITUM
THE MECHANICS OF POISON

It began with the bottles purchased at Jewel. More than one, less than five. The exact number wasn't clear. Dan was trying to hide them from me. There were enough bottles for him to experiment. Not enough to attract suspicion. Starter bottles stripped of innocence and repurposed inside the lair. Gloves were always worn because even a fingerprint could betray him. DNA was unknown in 1982.

The dispenser appeared harmless. Clear plastic, round, shaped like a rotary dial. Purchased at American Science & Surplus. It was marketed for vitamins or fishing tackle, never imagined as a device of murder. Or was it? Transparent body, circular face, 25 small holes hidden in plain sight. Each one measured, each one ratcheted forward with a mechanical click. A toy to the casual buyer, a precision instrument to Dan. A device of order and geometry. Its significance is only revealed when cyanide is spilled into the hollows and turns an innocent design into an architecture of death.

PILL DISPENSER

A nifty little gadget, the significance of which did not begin to depress us until much later. It's clear plastic and looks rather like a telephone dial. By rotating a metal clip in the base, one can separate the top from the bottom, thereby yielding access to 25 ¼" dia. by ¼" deep holes, numbered, not surprisingly, from 1 to 25.

Replace the top with the arrow aligned to the one blank hole in the thing, and you're ready to dispense. The gadget will ratchet in only one direction. Ratchet it one click, and a hole in the top lines up with bin 25 from below, and you can drop the contents into your hand, mouth, coffee, or waste basket. Made by American Hospital Supply for Uncle Sam. The most innocent use we've concocted is to use it for fly fishermen to put those pesky split shot lead weights in and to drop them into their hands (or fish) as they're needed.

THE MATHEMATICS OF DEATH

Each hole measured a quarter inch across and a quarter inch deep, yielding a volume of 0.201 cubic centimeters, the equivalent of 0.201 milliliters. A space small enough to look harmless yet vast enough to carry destruction. When filled with potassium cyanide, the density is measured at 1.52 grams per cubic centimeter. The weight of poison in each chamber reached approximately 306 milligrams.

The fatal dose for an adult hovers between 200 and 300 milligrams. Sometimes less, depending on body weight, metabolism, or the sheer cruelty of chance. One chamber surpassed that threshold. One click of the dispenser equaled certainty.

The capsules themselves fit the equation with precision that felt designed. Extra Strength Tylenol, in 1982, was red-and-white shells 0.90 inches long and 0.30 inches wide. They were hollow once split. Ready to be filled. Their dimensions aligned with the dispenser's output in near-perfect symmetry. The capsule could swallow the contents of the hole with room to spare, enough to hold multiple clicks, enough to contain multiple funerals within one shell.

Each capsule became a grave. Each bottle became an arsenal. The geometry was flawless. The math was merciless.

THE METHODICAL PROCESS

The ritual unfolded without deviation. Gloves drawn tight, dispenser filled, the arrow aligned. One click, one hole prepared, powder dropped through the hollow and into the capsule. The lock pick slipped the halves apart. Acetaminophen was scraped away, white powder discarded, cyanide poured in its place. The halves were pressed together again. The seam was inspected, the surface unbroken, no scar visible. No clue betrayed. The magnifying lamp hovered above, fluorescent light bleaching the table. Precision assured, illusion complete.

The capsules didn't return directly to the bottles. They waited first in bullet trays, small plastic grids meant for handloading. Rows designed to hold bullets upright, now pressed into service for poison. He lined the capsules in perfect formation, red-and-white shells gleaming under the lamp. Each one upright, each one stable, no rolling across the table, no spillage, no disorder. The trays transformed the capsules into ammunition, neat rows of death, each one identical, each one primed. The sight carried weight, a field of cartridges waiting for a weapon, medicine converted into bullets. Order masking horror.

He worked row by row. Each capsule was filled. Each capsule was resealed. The tray advanced like a conveyor of ritual. The rhythm of murder was steady and quiet. Once the rows were complete, he inspected again. The lamp revealed no imperfection, the seal flawless, the disguise absolute. From the tray, the capsules returned to newly awaiting bottles one by one. Placed with deliberation, no haste, no randomness.

Delivery of the new bottles was to be completed during the boys' weekend.

Cellucotton was pressed tight above them, fibers wedged to freeze the capsules in place. No shifting, no rattling, no sound to betray what had been done. The poisoned capsules rested near the top, positioned for the first hand, the first swallow, the first death.

THE CALCULATED EFFICIENCY

Every detail was measured, nothing improvised, no wasted movement. The dispenser held nearly twice the lethal dose in each chamber. The capsules held multiple doses with ease. The bullet trays provided order and stability. The magnifying lamp erased flaws. The cellucotton anchored the poisoned pills in silence.

Murder disguised as order. Death assembled with patience. Poison packed with precision.

Poisons offer a quiet alternative to things that go *boom* in the night…

SECTION SIX

CHAPTER EIGHT: DARK SECRETS

FEBRUARY 1988

I had matured quite a bit at this point. Sixteen. I was spending as much time away from Gage Avenue as possible and whenever possible, with my friend Tina. Tina believed in me before I knew that was even an option.

The cold in Chicago had a way of tightening its grip, even indoors. February always felt merciless. You could bet money that whatever weekend the Super Bowl was, that would be the coldest weekend in Chicago.

I had just stepped from the shower, steam still clinging to my skin. The house was quiet, muffled. My footsteps carried me toward my room, but I hesitated at the corner. Something felt wrong.

I leaned forward. Watched.

There he was. Lurking. Hands shifting through what wasn't his. My space. My air.

Oh fuck, what does he want? My thought, sharp as the frost outside.

He raised his head, eyes snagging mine. "Oh. Hi, Joe."

"Hi, Joe?" What is this?

He left the room without explanation. I moved quickly, dressed, heart still jittering. My ritual was simple: finish in the salon chair, outside the lair, outside the reach of his shadow. I sat down, hoping for calm. Instead, he was there. Waiting. Watching.

Dan stared. Not a word. Not a blink. Something about him felt off. So off. He carried it like a weight, yet his eyes stayed fixed on me.

Finally, he spoke.

"It's nice you go out with your friends. I've never been a very social type."

My mind hissed. *Yeah. Most psychos aren't.*

I studied him. He seemed unsteady, maybe drunk. He had never been a big drinker. Still, I could tell.

"Yeah, it's good you get out. You know, I've never told you, but you're a good-lookin' kid. Don't break too many hearts."

His voice was gentle. Almost fatherly. Tender words dressed in menace. All I could think about was Tina. Where was she? She was always late.

"Yeah. You don't want to end up like me."

No shit, my thought cut back. *Where the fuck is Tina?*

Then he said it. Flat. Quiet. A confession carried on stale breath. "I've killed people."

The air froze between us.

I paused for a moment. Thinking. Now I wanted to get comfortable. It was Tina's turn to wait. "Oh, you mean in Vietnam, right?" I forced the question.

"No. Not necessarily. My job in Vietnam was to save lives. Diffuse bombs. I did my share of saving lives back then." His words rolled very slowly and very matter-of-factly.

He leaned in closer.

"I cut the last wire on the last explosive device I disarmed the minute you were born."

My stomach twisted. My voice was unsteady. "Okay, then what do you mean when you say you've killed people?"

"You know, I'm not completely mentally stable."

I stared. *Really? You're kidding. I had no fucking idea.*

"I think I may be off in the head a little. Maybe from ingesting that sulfa when I was little. Maybe from the things I saw in the war. Or maybe I'm just off. Who the fuck knows?"

My pulse raced. My voice barely held. "You know they make medication for those things now, right?" Prozac was just reaching the shelves.

"I can't. If my work found out—and they would find out—they'd fire me."

I pressed. "I don't think that would happen. So, back to my question… Who did you kill?"

His reply came softly. Almost tender. Almost cruel.

"It's not important. You may figure it out someday. Or maybe you won't. Don't worry about it."

And then, salvation. The bell. The doorbell. Tina. Saved by the bell.

Or was I?

THE NEXT DAY

The house was silent when I slipped in after midnight. Too silent. My mother had left the door unlocked again. She always did. She said she couldn't rest until her children were home. She believed danger lived outside. She never knew the greater threat already breathed inside.

I went downstairs. I got ready for bed.

Morning came. I woke. Something felt wrong. Something was missing. Not one thing. Two.

The first was my journal that I had carefully hidden between the headboard and the wall. Gone.

I had filled those pages with what I saw. What I endured. I thought I was keeping track of details. Small details. Nothing about life with him was small. Every entry had become evidence. A record. A testimony. My attempt to decode him.

That journal was gone. Missing.

He was in my room last night.

The second missing item was a book. A new release. I had torn into it. I was halfway through. Pages heavy with mystery. Then gone. Missing.

Two disappearances. Two silences.

Both items carried weight. My words. My witness. My account of what I saw. Stolen. That book, a retelling of another crime. A mirror. A foreshadow.

Not chance. Not a coincidence. He was burying something. Erasing what linked him to it.

The journal held my truth. The book held his reflection. Their absence left a void. A void heavy with the shape of a crime not yet discovered.

THURSDAY, JUNE 6, 2013

My baby sister died this morning. A blood clot led to an embolism. An embolism led to death. That was it. She was gone.

She was my sister. My friend. My confidante. Some would say my ride or die.

Taken in an instant.

Her pain had begun years earlier. Her body was a battlefield. Surgery after surgery. Never an answer. Doctors dismissed her suffering as psychological. She numbed the pain with hydrocodone.

She pressed forward. She found marriage. She even bought a house only doors away on Gage Avenue, a step that should have promised peace. Instead, it bound her close to him. She told me she didn't want to leave our mother. She told me she didn't want to leave her alone. Alone with him. She confessed this to me often.

She lived in fear. Fear of truth. Fear of what truth would do. She worried that if she spoke the words aloud, our fragile family would collapse. Her silence became her prison.

She filled journals. She stacked books. She tried to place her pain on paper. She pressed forward with fragile hope. She knew those journals might vanish if she revealed them too soon. She had seen mine vanish. She feared hers would meet the same fate.

Now she was gone.

I loved her. I looked out for her the best I could. I would have taken a bullet for her without pause. She knew this. We had built a friendship beyond blood. A bond forged in secrets. In whispers. In pain.

2015

Drama still clung to Gage Avenue. Always more drama.

I had been planning a trip to Chicago. I wanted to see friends. I wanted to see family.

I had built a new life. I met my husband in 2002. We built a beautiful life together. We moved to California in 2014, after Liz died. I couldn't face another frozen winter without her.

I no longer had a relationship with Dan. Hard to imagine, yet true. What was left of that relationship was about to rupture.

"Danny doesn't want you to come home," my mom said during a phone call. Her voice cracked. She cried as she spoke.

"What is his problem? Put him on the phone," I answered.

"No. He doesn't want to talk to you."

What the fuck?

"He wants me to choose between you and him. I will not, though," she whispered.

This is crazy. What is his problem?

Age had twisted him even more. He had grown paranoid. He stockpiled guns. He filled closets with ammunition. He stacked powdered food. God only knew what else.

I saw it then. I was out of his orbit. He hated it. He could no longer control me from a distance. A black hole of a soul doesn't ever want to let anyone out of their orbit. He knew I knew things.

He knew I carried pieces of him inside my memory. The pieces hadn't yet aligned, yet they were sharp. Getting sharper.

After the phone call, Craig, my husband, reminded me of something. Something that I had buried.

He reminded me about Liz saying that she was scared. Sacred to start a new therapy program. Scared about what would happen when and if the truth came out. She gave no details.

Liz had been in an inpatient unit. No one from the family went to see her, except us. She had attempted suicide. I was well aware that her suicide attempt was a cry for help. A cry for what help?

Craig and I put the pieces together. When Liz was in that inpatient unit, she looked me in the eye and said, "There are things you don't know about. Nobody knows. Not even [her husband]."

I knew exactly who to call, a friend she had made during therapy. A friend whom she trusted with her secrets. A friend who had Liz's books and journals.

I made the call. S., her friend said, "I've been waiting for this call."

"Imagine my surprise when I walked into Lizzy's memorial service and saw HIM pontificating.

"She didn't want this information out yet. She didn't even want [Liz's husband] to know until she. Was. Ready.

"Your sister trusted me with her thoughts. She knew when the time was right that they would end up where they needed to be. I think the time is right."

Then the dark truth came. The darkest secret. Dan had been raping my sister from the time she was six until she turned thirteen.

That was why he didn't want me back. That was why he feared my voice. That was why he wanted silence. He knew I'd had words with Liz's husband after she died. He feared a spark. He feared a kerfuffle. He feared exposure.

I carried his secrets. He knew it. Now I carried this one.

However, I wasn't towing the family line and keeping this one quiet.

A confrontation happened. Dan neither confirmed nor denied. Just hung up.

It was that day that I cut him out of my life like a cancer. With surgical precision.

OCTOBER 19, 2019

I have had zero interaction with Dan. He still tried to control me via my mom. She wouldn't choose. He made her life a living hell every time she came to California for a visit.

Questions abound. Why didn't she leave him after nursing school? That was the plan. Why didn't she leave him after hearing the truth about the rape?

Maybe it was the idea of *until death do us part*. Maybe not. I cannot say.

I, however, have decided to strip any identity of his away from myself. Today I legally changed my last name.

DECEMBER 27, 2019

Dan has figured out that I changed my name. A black hole doesn't like it when you're out of their orbit. He sent this correspondence to me through Craig's Facebook.

> You can run but you can't hide JR.
> Hope to see you soon.
>
> Have a happy Nee Year. It will be the
> last for you.

JR=Joseph Robert.

AUGUST 6, 2023

Craig and I were out picking out furniture for our lake home. I was sending pictures to my mom. She was responding.

Craig was watching over my shoulder. "Who are you texting?" he asked.

"My mom. I'm sending her pics of the new furniture. Why?"

"No reason. Is she responding back?"

"Yes, she's responding. Why?"

"No reason. Let's just get this furniture bought and get a delivery date set up."

It was so strange that he was watching over my shoulder. *Oh well,* I thought. I chatted with the saleswoman for about 10 minutes. I'm a talker.

Once we got in the car, Craig said, "I thought you would never stop talking to her [the saleswoman]. I got a message while we were in the store from your mom. She wanted me to tell you... your dad has stage four pancreatic cancer. I'm sorry, Joey."

"What? Why didn't she just tell me instead of commenting on how much she liked the furniture? How good it will look in the house."

Okay, Joey. Wow. I love the furniture. It will look great. Did that couch come in other colors or fabrics? I love that chair. Oh yeah, I forgot to tell you, your father is dying, he has stage four pancreatic cancer. No hope for him. Can't wait to see the furniture in the house.

I had a lot of emotions. Understandably. I had the thought once again that maybe, just maybe, we could have a regular conversation. Maybe he would acknowledge the things he had done. Maybe I could forgive him.

No. None of that happened. Except that I did forgive him. Not for him, but for me. The energy spent hating someone is too much. It wasn't even that I hated him. I had become indifferent.

That was it. Indifferent.

A few days later, Craig showed me Daddy Dearest's correspondence from Facebook. He had kept it from me. I wasn't angry at that. Craig wasn't used to family dynamics quite like these.

Craig showed me the messages, and I took some time to reflect. I decided to reply to my father.

SEPTEMBER 19, 2023 – TEN DAYS BEFORE DAN'S DEATHBED DECLARATION

In response to your previous correspondence:

I wish you well on your journey.

I pray for nothing more than for you to use your final time to reflect and to find some peace.

I have forgiven you for all of your atrocities committed against me. Not for your sake. But for my sake.

This forgiveness has led me to freedom.

The poison that spilled from your spirit spread through everything it touched. It withered love. It corroded trust. It turned our home into a shadow. Yet from that same poison, I have drawn strength. I have drawn hope.

The ruin you left behind has not left me as an urn of ashes. It has given me a life sharpened by loss yet filled with meaning and love. I now know that urn holds more than memory. It holds silence.

For these things, I thank you. I have become a great man. I have become a successful man. Not because of you, but in spite of you.

Now this family will be moving forward.

We will no longer live under your reign of terror. I will carry this family into the future with dignity, with grace, with love, and with truth.

Your Son, Joey

LATER THAT DAY

I never got a response from Dan until his deathbed declaration. Secrets, lies, and codes. They now belonged to me. His training prepared me for this strange inheritance.

I spoke to my mother today. She told me how crushing it was. How crushing it had been when she heard Justin weeping in the shower, fists striking the wall, his voice breaking with the words, "Superman is dying. Superman is dying."

Still more waits in the shadows. More than I can measure. Questions multiplying. Answers vanishing. The truth doesn't rest.

And yet there is more. Much more. Always more questions than answers.

AUGUST 27, 2025 – MY MOM'S CONFESSION

I had a very long conversation with my mom today. We clearly have a lot to talk about. I wanted to talk to her about my dad's time in the military. While I was researching and interviewing for this book, a former co-worker of my dad's—we'll call him Ted—told me something that made the hair on the back of my neck stand up.

I knew that Ted and my father had been close. I tracked Ted down and we talked and set up an interview, and Ted gave me a lot of insight into my father. And just to be fair, Ted told me a few good things that he knew about my father too.

I didn't inform Ted—nor anyone else, for that matter—what case I was investigating. At the end of the conversation, I asked him, "Do you have any idea what I'm researching?"

Ted paused and then answered, "No. But if I were you, I would get your dad's military records. You might find some interesting things in there. Also, there is one more thing you need to know. **Your father had a *deep* knowledge of chemicals and chemistry."**

Ted told me how to get the military records from the National Archives, which I did.

I asked my mom about my father's time in the military. She told me that he had been given a *special* deal. Instead of the typical three-year enlistment, they would let him have a two-year enlistment. There was just one caveat.

While he was in Oakland, CA he went off the grid. All records about his time in Oakland were completely redacted. Pages of black.

I asked my mom about this *special* deal and his time in Oakland. She stated that my father was entering the military under the guise of EOD (Explosive Ordnance Disposal). But this wasn't completely accurate.

Yes, my father did EOD training. My mom confirmed that. However, he also trained as an assassin. Both as a sniper and… **with poisons.**

That checks out with the stories that he had previously told me.

The sad part is that when he left the military, he promised her that he had left that life behind.

And yet there is more. Much more. Always more questions than answers.

CHAPTER NINE: THE END OF THE BEGINNING

WHITE AVENUE

It's Yesterday Once More

I was born on 7/17/1971 at 1:11 a.m. A perfect string of sevens and ones. It sounds poetic, even magical.

We lived on White Avenue then. 8141 White Avenue, third floor, front apartment. I was too young to remember much, just a scattering of moments, like shards of glass on a dirty floor. But one memory stands out. It always has. I must have been around three. It was the first time I felt the world shift beneath me. My dad was in a bathrobe, lounging on the floor between our itchy green couch and the coffee table. The air was thick, quiet. He had a small bookcase nearby, one of the few constants in our existence. Burgundy, hunter green, gold, and brown filled its shelves. The bookshelf opened to show a glass decanter and a few tiny shot glasses resting like relics on display. I remember all of this because that bookcase followed us.

That night, or was it day? Yes, it was daytime. He was pouring something dark and purplish out of the decanter and into the shot glass. He was alone but talking out loud. Maybe to himself. Maybe to me. Maybe to something I couldn't see.

I was barely walking. I shuffled over, wrapped in my own childhood curiosity and innocence. I asked, in baby gibberish, what he was doing.

He didn't answer. He just smiled in that half-interested way he did when he had other things on his mind. Then he poured some of the liquid into a shot glass, sat me on the floor next to him, opened my mouth, and poured it down my throat.

It burned, like swallowing fire. I remember the heat. I remember the taste. I remember the smell. I remember nothing after that.

I think I passed out. I remember the couch and then nothing. No ending to the scene. No gentle fade. Just a cut to black.

And that's how my life began.

We left White for Gage Avenue on Memorial Day weekend in 1976. Hopeful. Naïve. Unaware that "Gage Avenue" would soon become a phrase I would associate with dread.

But at first, things were good. My dad acted like a superhero. Part builder, part dreamer. He built me a custom clubhouse, a treehouse with a working phone line, and a sandbox. Shortly thereafter, he installed a Chicago-style above-ground pool. All the who's who in Lyons had one. Life felt full, even if I didn't know how temporary that fullness was. I had nearly forgotten about the booze incident on White Ave. Almost. But not completely.

Easter 1978. We were headed south in a powder blue Chevy Vega, the eight-track humming Karen Carpenter's sultry, velvety voice like a lullaby. We were heading to Grandma's house on Vine Street in Chillicothe, Missouri. It was an annual exodus. Mom packed the car with perms to ensure that no niece, aunt, or neighbor went without fresh curls.

We would cruise south on I-55, stop for pancakes at the Dixie Truck Stop, and feast on peanut butter, syrup, and sticky laughter. Pittsfield, Illinois, became a sacred marker, our traditional lunch stop. Denny's, gas stations, green fields... then the caves of Hannibal. We went so often that I cannot even count the trips. It was muscle memory by the time I turned seven.

I would doze in the back seat until we pulled up to Grandma's white four-square on Vine Street. That house was a time capsule: green shag carpet, orange linoleum, and enough cousins to start a minor league baseball team.

I'll never forget the feeling of running through Grandma's door and seeing my cousin Karen. She had grown since I last saw her. No longer a kid, now fully radiant. Karen loved kids. She especially loved me. But to get to her, I had to navigate one final obstacle: her little sister, my cousin Sherrie. She accidentally stuck her foot out as I rushed to Karen's arms. Typical.

A few years earlier, Sherrie had taken me to the park around the corner from Grandma's house. We loaded up on baseball-shaped bubble gum and sugar high dreams. We walked and talked until we reached the monkey bars. She dared me to climb. Then she bolted across the street. She didn't even look both ways. She yelled back, "See you later, shithead."

I screamed. My gum fell from my mouth in cinematic slow motion. I clambered down the bars, ran across the street, and never forgave her.

Until I did.

That night, after humiliating me by making me dress up in pantyhose and a wig on my head to "Disco Duck" (I secretly didn't mind), Sherrie let me fall asleep in her lap. Later, in a moment of pure three-year-old clarity, I bit her thigh. A scar remains.

I believe that these were probably some of the last and few good memories in my family.

SEPTEMBER 30, 1978 – THE TURNING POINT

My mom was cleaning cabinets in our kitchen when she was overtaken by the strong scent of flowers. Odd. She paused, thought of Karen, and continued cleaning out the cabinets like it was any other Saturday. Nothing more happened; at least, not then.

That night, she had a dream:

A phone call came through. A voice said, "Mary Grace, you don't need to worry about her. She's okay. She's with me." My mom asked, "Who?" The voice replied, "Your niece, Karen." "Who is this?" she asked. The voice, soft and certain, said, "Daddy."

Then the call ended.

"Daddy" is what my mom called her father, my grandfather, Clarence. He had passed away in 1974, but his presence still echoed through our home.

The morning after my mom's dream, the phone actually did ring. This time, it was real. My Aunt Carol, my mom's sister, called in hysterics, wailing, gasping. Karen had been in a car crash. It was homecoming night. She had been riding with friends when their car collided head-on with a drunk driver just outside Independence, Missouri. All four teenagers died instantly. So did the other driver. It was sudden. Brutal. And the way the adults handled it in 1978 was essentially, *Karen is gone. Don't say her name. Move on.*

That was it. No therapy. No processing. No ceremony beyond hushed voices and a closed bedroom door. Karen was gone. And we were expected to pretend she had never existed.

Her death marked the beginning of the end of normal for us. Just a few weeks later, on October 15, 1978, my brother Justin was born. I was excited. Another little soul to travel this journey with. I knew that I wasn't alone.

But I'll be polite. Justin was a terror. Even before birth, he managed to break a few of my mom's ribs from the inside. He came out kicking. And screaming. And fighting. He never really stopped. Justin had been born into trauma.

AND THEN CAME SHERRIE

After Karen's death and our family's refusal to speak her name, Sherrie began to unravel. When the Missouri State Trooper arrived at their house to deliver the news, 14-year-old Sherrie grabbed a baseball bat and beat the shit out of the officer's car. I cannot say I blamed her. That was how we dealt with grief back then—through silence, violence, or both.

The next step was to send her to us. My parents took her in. She lived with us in Chicago for a time. I loved and hated her being there. We laughed together, and we bonded in our trauma. But Karen's name never passed her lips. Not once. Not even now.

Sherrie drifted in and out of our home. Her presence was a reminder of everything lost. And 1978? It wasn't done with us yet.

That November, the Jonestown massacre occurred. I didn't understand it. Not fully. But my father? He was obsessed. Completely consumed by it.

Jonestown wasn't just a massacre. It was a contagion of death. Jim Jones had taken over 900 souls. Mothers, babies, and elders were convinced to drink poison-laced Kool-Aid. Cyanide. My dad couldn't stop watching the coverage. Couldn't stop talking about it. The way Jones had chosen poison fascinated him. He secretly had newspaper clippings that he kept in his workshop.

After the light of my first years, darkness came fast. Karen's death. Justin's colicky wails. Sherrie's heartbreak. And Jonestown, broadcast over every channel. My father, who once built treehouses and swung me to the sky, began to shift. He wasn't the same man anymore.

Relationships are never black or white. And my relationship with my father was no exception. The first seven years of my life had been filled with some trauma, but there was love. 1978 changed him. It changed us all.

Alongside his day job at Electro-Motive, my father was also a police officer and a volunteer firefighter in Lyons. I remember, I was probably three years old. He climbed up the ladder on the water tower next to the fire department with me strapped to his back in a baby backpack. All the way to the top. I was quiet and still. He was a hero to some. Brave, even. But there was another side to him that crept in slowly. And then all at once.

Sometimes, with Sherrie in the car, he would attach a blue strobe light to the roof and speed down Harlem Avenue. For show. For control. He would whip out nunchucks and spin them inches from Sherrie's face. He also pulled the loaded gun on Sherrie. It was his version of intimidation. His way of asserting dominance.

I didn't know how to make sense of him. He scared me. But then… there was *Star Wars*.

It became our demilitarized zone. Since 1977, he had taken me to see it over 30 times. Right after Justin was born, he even brought me to the Museum of Science and Industry to see the Star Wars robots. For a brief moment, I had my dad back. Gentle. Present. Proud.

That trip, walking up to R2D2 and C3PO, was the last slice of peace I remember before everything shifted once again.

By the end of 1978, something inside my father had hardened. He had always been tough, maybe even mean. But now he was angry. Unpredictable. Violent. And that was a new kind of fear for me.

1979

As the decade began to close, so did the version of my father I had once known. He was no longer the patient man who built swing sets. He was becoming someone else entirely. Someone cruel.

He had a special punishment just for me. It was called "flick your pee-pee." He would scold me and make me drop my pants, exposing myself. He would take his thumb and middle finger to make a *flick* and flick the tip of my penis. It hurt. It was embarrassing. It was humiliating. It was a punishment he would administer only when nobody else was around. He would taunt me with it when other people were around, though. He would jokingly say, "I'll flick your pee-pee." People thought he was kidding. People actually laughed. It has taken me 45 years to even unpack that.

Justin cried constantly. He never stopped. Some people called it colic. But to me, he was just a terror. Screaming. Wailing. Every second. Every day.

One Saturday, my father snapped.

He barged into the room I shared with Justin. Snatched Justin up. Shook him hard, then slammed him back down into the crib.

I froze.

Our mom rushed in, horrified. "Leave that baby alone!" she shouted.

My dad turned on her and screamed, "You fucking bitch, don't you dare go in there and coddle him!"

That was the first time I saw *real* violence with my own eyes. Unfortunately, it wouldn't be the last.

Life on Gage got darker. My father's rage spilled over everywhere. I didn't want to go anywhere with him. His excursions became nightmares.

BUT THE WORST CAME LATER

I had a loose tooth. I was eight.

We had been at an open house at Robinson School that evening. My dad had been funny, charming, and entertaining at the open house. Walking home after, I had a feeling of contentedness. Like maybe his violent outbursts were something temporary. Maybe an adjustment period after all of the life-changing events of 1978.

Well, hope springs eternal.

My loose tooth bothered me, but I figured it would fall out on its own. My father had other ideas. He approached me with a small pair of pliers.

Yes, pliers. I said, "No."

He said, "Sit."

He laid me across his lap, holding me down with one arm. He forced my mouth open with the other and began probing around for the tooth. My heart pounded. I was shaking.

He found it. Clamped down. Yanked.

The sound was awful. Ripping. Cracking. My mouth filled with blood. I tumbled to the floor, stunned and weak. My eyes welled with tears, but I couldn't cry. I wouldn't cry. I wasn't going to give him the satisfaction. As I looked up at him, I saw something behind his eyes that haunts me to this day.

Rage. Pure rage.

I ran to the bathroom to rinse my mouth. I was eight fucking years old.

What could I do?

1980

The year brought more of the same, a maddening carousel of volatility and tension. The outbursts were no longer isolated; they were escalating, wrapping tightly around our lives like a noose. My survival increasingly depended on honing my powers of observation. I had become a student of subtle cues: a clenched jaw, the sound of footsteps, the rhythm of a breath just before it snapped into fury. Hypervigilance wasn't a choice. It became an instinct.

In August, we embarked on what was supposed to be a dream vacation, a family trip to Hawaii. For most, Hawaii conjures images of *paradise*. For us, it was a *paradox*—beauty on the outside, dread beneath. Going to Hawaii should have been a dream. Mr. Drozd made even the most tranquil beaches feel like a nightmare when he was near. My grandma and Sherrie had flown in from Missouri to go with us. Thank God for that. Grannie's presence was more than comforting. It was hopeful, at least temporarily. He never showed his true colors around her. He knew better. She wasn't someone he could manipulate or bully. Her presence served as a buffer, holding back the worst of him like a dam holding back a flood.

There were moments, however brief, of joy. We laughed, especially when he wasn't around. When he did appear, it was as if someone had unplugged the sun. His presence sucked the life, light, and warmth out of everything. Still, we got through it. We always did, but it left an indelible mark.

This is the time in my memory when Dan started to take me on these strange hikes.

He taught me what plants were edible. A completely useful topic, except that in the same breath, he was teaching me which plants were poisonous. Again, very useful. It was his commentary after discussing the poison plants that was disturbing.

He would describe to me, in great detail, how to use these poison plants. Yes. How to use them to kill. He put a lot of thought into the details of how to dry them. How to use them in tea for an enemy.

How to add them to food.

He taught me how to stalk in the woods. "Walk silently with purpose. Watch where you step and be sure not to make a sound. Always be aware of everything in front of you. To your left. To your right. Keep track of what is behind you. Always look up. Always stick to the left."

He started trying to teach me how to use a watch as a compass, an idea that I never understood.

By December, the patterns were undeniable. His moods, once unpredictable, had become clockwork. More frequent and more severe. I could chart the tension like a snowstorm preparing to hit Chicago. By my mother's birthday in December, everything had begun to crack. Justin's face and body bore the evidence of multiple bruises. There was the awful memory of us celebrating my mom's birthday while she wore a black eye like a new birthday sweater.

By Christmas, the dam broke.

The screams. The shattered ornaments. The silence that followed. The kind of silence that isn't peaceful but oppressive. The type of silence that knows too much, that bids one to beware.

The end of the beginning. The beginning of the end.

And yet there is more. Much more. Always more questions than answers.

EPILOGUE

Learning who our father truly was has given something rare to all of us: closure. Closure for the families of the victims. Closure for our family. Closure for me. In a space engineered for darkness, I have found hope. Hope for a better future. Hope for a place where victims' families, my family, and I can have peace.

I was a month shy of four years old in September of 1982, yet that year burns brighter in my memory than most of my childhood. Any account in these pages where I appear, I remember with startling detail. We were taught to be observant by our father. Or because of him. "Always be aware of everything in front of you. To your left. To your right. Keep track of what is behind you. Always look up. Always stick to the left."

I loved my father. I feared him. I still love him, which is why this hurts. He was complicated. Layered. A man with many sides. He showed the world one version of himself and saved his truest versions for those closest to him. For his family. His mood could shift without warning. One moment warm. The next something entirely different.

He taught me things. Good things. Bad things. I absorbed all of it like a sponge.

He taught me violence.
He taught me how to save lives.
He taught me arson.
He taught me how to extinguish fire.
He taught me poisonous plants.
He taught me medicinal ones.

Always duality. Always light. Always dark. And between them, the gray.

He used to tell me about the gray man. "Stay quiet. Don't stand out. Blend into your surroundings. Be the gray."

Those lessons became a lifelong push and pull. A tension inside me. A constant negotiation between who he wanted me to be, who he taught me to be, and who I chose to become. The truth is simple: Throughout my childhood and into my adult life I've battled my own personal demons while at the same time trying my best to do good. I've suffered crippling depression, violence, addiction, and loss of some of those closest to me. At the same time, I've found hope. A wedge was driven between my brother and me and for years, we didn't speak. I blame my father for this.

And as I've said before, I loved my father. I still do. I've hoped and prayed that he didn't commit these crimes. But the things he said to me in the last years of his life, and the things he said as he was dying, opened more questions than answers. Always more. More questions than answers. They linger. They unsettle. They refuse to resolve.

When this book first began, I wanted nothing to do with it. I shut down. I refused to speak to my brother. The weight of it felt too heavy. The truth felt too sharp. If it were not for a dear friend guiding me through the emotions, reminding me that my silence would follow me, haunt me, shape me for the rest of my days, I don't know that I would be writing this now.

Thank you, Elena.

This story marks an ending. But for me, it also marks a beginning.

My beginning.

—Justin Drozd, December 11, 2025

BIBLIOGRAPHY

Axelrod, David. "Tyrone and Tylenol." *Chicago Tribune*, October 16, 1982.

Beck, Melinda, with Sylvester Monroe in Ft. Washington, Mary Hager in Washington, & Ron LaFramboise. "The Tylenol Scare." *Newsweek*, October 11, 1982, United States Edition, National Affairs, 32.

Chicago Tribune. "In a Handwritten Note to The Chicago Tribune, the Man Sought Nationwide as an Extortion Suspect in the Tylenol Poisoning Deaths Claims Neither He nor His Wife Was Responsible." October 31, 1982.

Greene, Bob. "Dear Madman." *Chicago Tribune*, October 18, 1982.

Koziol, Ronald, & John O'Brien. "Tylenol Note Suspect Hunted: Detectives Uncover Link to 1978 Murder in Kansas City." *Chicago Tribune*, October 15, 1982.

"Tylenol Suspect Volatile, Probers Say." *Chicago Tribune*, October 17, 1982.

United Press International (UPI). "Chicago—Archbishop Joseph L. Bernardin Embraced Grieving Relatives." October 5, 1982.

REFERENCES CIBELLI ARTICLE

American Psychiatric Association. (2022). *Diagnostic and Statistical Manual of Mental Disorders* (5th ed., text rev.). American Psychiatric Publishing.

Blair, R. J. R., Mitchell, D. G. V., & Blair, K. S. (2005). *The Psychopath: Emotion and the Brain.* Oxford University Press.

Cohen, L. E., & Felson, M. (1979). Social change and crime rate trends: A routine activity approach. *American Sociological Review*, 44(4), 588–608.

Hare, R. D. (2003). The Hare Psychopathy Checklist–Revised (2nd ed.). Multi-Health Systems.

Hare, R. D., & Neumann, C. S. (2008). Psychopathy as a clinical and empirical construct. *Annual Review of Clinical Psychology*, 4, 217–246.

LoPachin, R. M., & Gavin, T. (2015). Toxic neuropathies: Mechanistic insights into axon and myelin injury. *Toxicologic Pathology*, 43(1), 19–35.

Merton, R. K. (1938). Social structure and anomie. *American Sociological Review*, 3(5), 672– 682.

Miller, J. D., Lynam, D. R., Hyatt, C. S., & Campbell, W. K. (2017). Controversies in narcissism. *Annual Review of Clinical Psychology*, 13, 291–315.

O'Brien, T., Bailey, M., & Bellomo, R. (2014). Neurological sequelae of diethylene glycol poisoning. *Neurotoxicology*, 44, 179–185.

Patrick, C. J., Fowles, D. C., & Krueger, R. F. (2009). Triarchic conceptualization of psychopathy: Developmental origins of disinhibition, boldness, and meanness. *Development and Psychopathology*, 21, 913–938.

Pincus, A. L., & Lukowitsky, M. R. (2010). Pathological narcissism and narcissistic personality disorder. *Annual Review of Clinical Psychology*, 6, 421–446.

Schep, L. J., Slaughter, R. J., Temple, W. A., & Beasley, D. M. G. (2009). Diethylene glycol poisoning. *Clinical Toxicology*, 47(6), 525–535.

Sutherland, E. H. (1947). *Principles of Criminology* (4th ed.). J. B. Lippincott.

Sykes, G. M., & Matza, D. (1957). Techniques of neutralization: A theory of delinquency. *American Sociological Review*, 22(6), 664–670.

Vize, C. E., Lynam, D. R., Collison, K. L., & Miller, J. D. (2020). The importance of antagonism in explaining the similarities and differences between grandiose narcissism and psychopathy. *Clinical Psychological Science*, 8(3), 1–14.

21 C.F.R. § 211.132 (Tamper-evident packaging requirements for over-the-counter human drug products).

18 U.S.C. § 1365 (Federal Anti-Tampering Act).

For More News About Joseph Cibelli,
Signup For Our Newsletter:

http://wbp.bz/newsletter

Word-of-mouth is critical to an author's long-term success. If you appreciated this book please leave a review on the Amazon sales page:

https://wbp.bz/tylenolmurders

www.ingramcontent.com/pod-product-compliance
Lightning Source LLC
Chambersburg PA
CBHW051500030726
47592CB00006B/2018